W9-CJZ-527

How We Fight for Our Lives

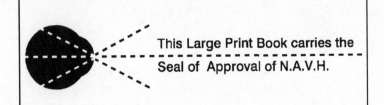

This Large Print Book carries the Seal of Approval of N.A.V.H.

How We Fight for Our Lives

A Memoir

Saeed Jones

THORNDIKE PRESS
A part of Gale, a Cengage Company

Copyright © 2019 by Saeed Jones.
"Elegy with Grown Folks' Music" by Saeed Jones first appeared in *Tin House* #69.
Thorndike Press, a part of Gale, a Cengage Company.

**LIBRARY OF CONGRESS CIP DATA ON FILE.
CATALOGUING IN PUBLICATION FOR THIS BOOK
IS AVAILABLE FROM THE LIBRARY OF CONGRESS**

ISBN-13: 978-1-4328-7523-7 (hardcover alk. paper)

Published in 2020 by arrangement with Simon & Schuster, Inc.

Printed in Mexico
Print Number: 01   Print Year: 2020

For Carol Jean Sweet-Jones

PRELUDE

Elegy with Grown Folks' Music

"I Wanna Be Your Lover" comes on the
    kitchen radio
and briefly, your mother isn't your
    mother —
just like, if the falsetto is just right, a black
    man in black
lace panties isn't a faggot, but a prince,
a prodigy — and the woman with your
    hometown
between her hips shimmies past the
    eviction notice
burning on the counter and her body
    moves like she never
even birthed you. The voice on the radio
    pleads
"I wanna be the only one that makes you
    come
running." Some songs take women places
    men cannot

7

follow. Spinning, she looks at but doesn't
  see you,
spinning, she sings lyrics too fast for you to
  pursue,
spinning, she doesn't have time for
  questions like:
What is this nasty song and where did she
  learn
to dance like *that* and *why,* and who is this
  high-pitched
bitch of a man who can sing like a woman
  and turn
your mother not into your mother but a
  woman,
not even a woman, but a box-braided black
  girl, a fast
girl, a chick, a Vanity 6 and how far away
  she is from you
right here in the same living room, dancing
with the song's hook in her throat. And
  you hate
the voice coming through the radio
  because another
sissy has snatched your dreams and
run off with them
and because you're young and don't know
  the difference
between abandoned and alone just like
  your mother's

heart won't know the difference between
   beat
and attack. She'll be dead in a decade and
   maybe
you already know what you're losing
   without knowing
how, but you're just a boy for now and
   your mother
is just a woman, just a girl, body swaying,
   fingers
snapping and snakes in her blood.

■ ■ ■ ■

Part One

■ ■ ■ ■

Since no one has talked to him about such feelings, he does not know what they are. And yet he is drawn to them, to the dream-like quality of doing something he has never done before, yet knowing, somehow, how to do it.

— DAVID MURA

1

May 1998
Lewisville, Texas

The waxy-faced weatherman on Channel 8 said we had been above 90 degrees for ten days in a row. Day after day of my T-shirt sticking to the sweat on my lower back, the smell of insect repellant gone slick with sunscreen, the air droning with the hum of cicadas, dead yellow grass cracking under every footstep, asphalt bubbling on the roads. It didn't occur to me to be nervous about the occasional wall of white smoke on the horizon that summer. Everything already looked like it was scorched, dead, or well on its way.

I was twelve years old and I had just finished the sixth grade. Most days, after Mom headed to her job at the airport, I would stay inside our apartment, stationed by the window. Cody and his younger brother, Sam, two white boys who lived a

13

few apartment buildings over from us, were always playing catch in the parking lot, though I never joined them. I wasn't good at throwing the ball and it was too hot for me to go out and pretend.

When I wasn't at my perch, acting like I wasn't watching them, I would flip through Mom's old paperback books. So far, I had tried out *Tar Baby* and *The Color Purple,* both unsuccessfully. Toni Morrison's sentences were like rivers with murky bottoms. They didn't obey the rules I was learning in school. When I stepped in, I couldn't see my feet; I retreated back to the shore. Alice Walker lost me because, a few pages in, some girl was talking about the color of her pussy. I figured the book didn't have much more to offer me after that.

Today I tried again. I picked up a worn copy of *Another Country* by James Baldwin, sat down cross-legged on the floor, and started reading. A sad man walks through the streets of New York City late one winter night. He goes into a jazz club looking for someone or something but doesn't say why.

Minutes pooled into hours. Black people sleeping with white people. Men kissing men, then kissing women, then kissing men again. Every few pages, I would look up from the book and peek at our apartment's front door. Mom wasn't home from work yet and I felt like I would get in trouble if she saw me reading this book. I went into my bedroom, with our cocker spaniel, Kingsley, trailing behind me, and I closed the door.

The novel turned me on. I didn't know books were capable of anything like this. Until now, I had liked reading but it was just something you did. A good thing, like drinking water on a hot day, but nothing special. Holding *Another Country* in my hands, I felt that the book was actually holding me. Sad, sexy, and reeking of jazz, the story had its arm around my waist. I could walk right into the scene, take off my clothes, and join one of the couples in bed. I could taste their tongues.

About a third of the way into the novel, I found a Polaroid tucked between the pages like a bookmark. It was a picture of a man I had never seen before. He didn't resemble anyone in my family, but, for all I knew, he could have been a distant cousin or uncle. He was leaning against a sedan with his arms crossed and an odd smile on his face, as if the person holding the camera had just told him an inside joke. Or maybe this man was doing the telling. The smile felt intimate, inappropriate, like a hand sliding down where it should not be.

Someone had written "Jackson, Mississippi, 1982" on the back, but I could've figured that out on my own. The man was dressed like an extra in a Michael Jackson video. He had on a knit sweater and black, acid-washed jeans that were way too tight. I could see the whites of his socks. And I knew he was in Mississippi because of the red dust all over his sneakers. On a trip to Mississippi with my aunt once, I'd seen that dirty redness on every car, lapping at the sides of houses like flood tides, and all over the loafers I was wearing. "That's what Mississippi does to you," my aunt had said when she saw my shoes. I kept on trying to use one foot to brush red dirt off the other, only making things worse.

I decided I didn't like the man in the picture. The dirt on his shoes irritated me, and the longer I looked at his smile, the more I felt like he was looking directly at me. Not at the camera in 1982, but at me, sixteen years later. He grinned like he knew something about me, a punch line I hadn't figured out yet.

When Mom came home from work, she headed straight into the kitchen to pour herself a glass of water from the Ozark jug. That was part of her routine. She'd drink

16

the entire glass right there in front of the fridge. Then she'd walk into her room and stare at the TV for a little bit, listening to the weatherman deliver a forecast — *more heat* — she already knew.

Mom was beautiful but always on the edge of exhaustion. When she was in her twenties, she had worked briefly as a fashion model. Sometimes she'd let me look at pictures of her from those days, hair in box braids, her lithe frame draped in gowns her sister had designed, posing on runways. Even a long day of work couldn't deny her the colors her black hair flashed, like raven feathers, when the light hit it just so. I was proud of her beauty, my first diva. Even as my body felt mangled by puberty, I took consolation in the fact that I came from a woman like her: a woman who read three newspapers every day, who could make everyone in a room light up with laughter, who would tuck notes into my lunch box daily, signing off, "I love you more than the air I breathe."

After working at the airport all day, Mom was too tired for any of my questions, so I waited until she'd had a cigarette. After a smoke, she would be ready to talk.

She saw the Polaroid in my hand when I walked up to her. "I'd been wondering what happened to that." She held the photo in her hand gently, as if it would crumble to dust if she wasn't careful. Her face softened just a little.

"Who is he?" I asked.

She looked out the window at the oak tree right outside the living room. She stared at it long and hard, like she was waiting for some signal. Moments like this had taught me how to shut up and wait for an answer. When I was younger, I would give up during Mom's pauses because I thought the answer wasn't going to come. Eventually I learned that she was just testing me, to see how serious I was about finding out.

I stared at the window with her, then arched one eyebrow.

She sighed.

"A friend from school. We'd go on road trips together now and then. We went to Jackson once."

She paused again, still looking at the tree. For a moment, it was quiet inside the apartment and out, like the heat was making the entire town hold its breath. Then Cody and Sam started yelling at each other in the parking lot.

Mom frowned and turned back to me.

"Not too long after that, he found out he was sick and . . . and he killed himself."

She was already walking back to the kitchen for more water, which was her way of saying that the conversation was over. It was too hot, the day too long.

I wanted to see the man's picture again. He had looked healthy to me. He was young, early twenties. And what did being sick have to do with killing yourself?

"Sick with what?" I called out, even as I felt bad for asking.

I had stepped into someone else's house without their permission, but now that I was inside I couldn't help looking around.

"AIDS," she said.

She breezed into her bedroom and closed the door. I could hear her open a drawer and turn the TV on. I tried to listen for the weatherman's predictions, but the volume was down too low.

I went back into my room and pulled *Another Country* out from under my pillow. After reading and rereading the same paragraph several times, I set the book back down.

AIDS, I thought. *Shit.*

She hadn't even said her friend's name.

"Gay" wasn't a word I could imagine actually hearing my mom say out loud. If I pictured her moving her lips, "AIDS" came

19

out instead. But in the days following our conversation about the photograph, I could feel the word "gay" — or maybe the word's conspicuous absence — vibrating in the air between us.

I'd read in one of my nature books that there are some sounds that occur at a frequency only dogs and special radios can pick up on. Sounds that can only be heard if you were designed to hear them. I could hear that word ringing high above every conversation, every moment, because I thought about being gay all the time.

I heard it vibrating in the air when I watched Cody and his friends playing pickup in the park, sweat making their shirts transparent and heavy, their nipples poking at the fabric. I could hear it too when I thought about the man in the photograph. I wished I still had the Polaroid, but it would've been weird to ask Mom if I could look at it again. I wanted to see his smile; I thought I would understand it better now.

I carried that man's smile in my head for three days until the smirk became a laugh, a taunt, a howl. One morning as Mom got ready to leave for work, I stared at the ceiling, then closed my eyes when she opened my bedroom door to let the dog in. Whenever she left, Kingsley would panic, pressing his face against the window so he could watch her car pull away. It happened five days a week; but each morning he was just as frantic, as if this would be the day she left, never to return.

With Kingsley yipping at my ankles, I ventured into Mom's room. The picture wasn't on her dresser and I thought about going through her drawers to find it. The last time I had done that, though, I'd found her vibrator. The discovery had been its own punishment.

Still, I knew that there was a place I could go to get the answers I wouldn't find at home. Throwing on clothes without even eating, I opened the front door and locked it behind me. Kingsley barked and scratched at the sill as if he were trying to warn me.

In the public library's air-conditioned coolness, I decided I knew better than to ask the wrinkled woman at the circulation desk where to find books about being gay. Instead, I slowly walked up and down each aisle, scanning book spines until I found what I was looking for. The first book that stopped me was for parents *dealing* with gay children. The introduction was worded like it was intended for readers coping with a late-stage cancer diagnosis. I put the book back on the shelf, wrong side out.

Eventually, I gathered five or six books and sat down on the floor with them in my lap. Like any teenage boy trained at reading things he shouldn't be, I looked both ways before opening any, then got up and grabbed a decoy off the shelf. It was a book about the "sociology of boys." I kept it open on the second chapter and within reach in case someone I knew came down the aisle and I needed a quick alibi.

While I was reading a book about "defining homosexuality," my dick started to get hard. The writing certainly wasn't sexy; the language was outdated and dry. Still my body responded.

That changed as I read further into the books in my pile. All the books I found about being gay were also about AIDS. Gay men dying of AIDS like it was a logical sequence of events, a mathematical formula, or a life cycle. Caterpillar, cocoon, butterfly; gay boy, gay man, AIDS. It was certain. Mom's friend got AIDS because he was gay. Because he was gay, he killed himself. Because he knew he was dying anyway.

I read about gay men who were abandoned by their families when they came out. Or worse, who didn't tell anyone that they were gay, even when lesions started to blossom on their skin like awful flowers. Either way, the men in those books always seemed to die alone. I took some comfort in the fact that Mom knew about her friend's illness. Maybe he had been able to tell the people close to him. Maybe Mom was the kind of person you could tell.

When I stood up to put the books back on the shelf, I realized my hands were shaking. I felt like I had made the mistake of asking a fortune-teller to look into my future, and now I was being punished for trying to look too far ahead. Walking outside, the blast of hot air was a relief.

I passed the park on the way home, and the usual boys were on the basketball court. Shirts and skins. I looked at their bodies, but only for a moment. I couldn't really focus. In every man's expression, shimmering amid the heat waves, I found myself searching for the face of the man in the photograph — for a hint of that smile, that beautiful, unforgivable smile.

2

June 1998
Lewisville, Texas

By the time Cody asked me if I wanted to go with him and his brother into the woods near our apartment complex, I had already been humping my pillow and whispering his name in breathy gasps for weeks.

I'd been in my bedroom, reading another book from Mom's bookshelf — this time Tina Turner's autobiography — when Cody knocked on the door. I thought the invitation was a trick at first, the lead-up to some prank. Part of me still felt that way as we walked toward the woods.

"You're not gonna believe it, man. He's built a hut and everything," said Cody.

"Fuck!" added Sam, who had a tendency of punctuating anything his older brother said with a curse word.

We posted up under a giant crepe myrtle tree to take in a moment of shade. Cody

24

hocked a loogie, then we ventured out into the heat. Really, I could've cared less about this crazy man and his hut; I was just excited to get to be around Cody.

Even though he was scrawny and had more acne than me, Cody was popular at school. He could sit wherever he wanted at lunch (except with the black kids); I sat with the band kids and tried to discreetly avoid sitting with the table of black kids, who if given half a chance would lay into me with one joke after another. Once I'd gotten so upset at them, during a ten-minute barrage about the khaki pants Mom insisted I wear, that I hollered, "And you call yourself a Christian!" Which only made everyone laugh louder. I could understand why Cody would pretend not to know me, as if we didn't see each other every day on the steps of our apartments.

"Hell yeah!" shouted Sam as if he heard what I was thinking. Sam grabbed a tree branch off the ground and held it above his head like a spear. With his buck teeth and freckles, he looked like one of the maniac schoolboys from *Lord of the Flies,* except with a Texas accent.

"Put that shit down," said Cody, talking around the Blow Pop lodged in his right cheek. "We're not gonna kill him, Sam."

The fact that Cody even had to clarify this to his brother worried me.

"Well, what are we gonna do?" I asked. "Gonna" instead of "going to" took effort; I was my mother's son.

Cody stopped walking and leaned toward me. I could smell the Blow Pop's green apple flavor on his breath. Having him so close made me nervous, as if I might kiss him by accident. I took a small step back.

"We're gonna huff and puff and blow his house down," he said, leaning in farther. His voice was low, hovering between menace and seduction.

"We're gonna —" I sputtered. "What?"

Cody sighed and dug around in his pockets, probably looking for another Blow Pop. "We're gonna tear down the old man's hut."

"Fuck yeah!" added Sam.

"Why?" I felt like a punk for even asking.

Both brothers sucked their teeth at the question and walked away without a word, as if I'd let them down. I knew the answer all right. We were bored. It was hot. And there was nothing better to do than break things.

No one would admit it, but we were nervous and underprepared. A few yards into the trees, we realized that our tennis shoes —

already falling apart — were no match for the brambles and cacti hidden in the thick grass. We didn't talk much because we were busy wincing, dodging thorns, and looking out for madman-shaped shadows. Our view of the brick apartment buildings was soon eclipsed by tree branches. The sun's glare was replaced by pockets of shadow. We heard birds and somewhere, out of sight, the gurgle of a little creek.

Eventually, we made it within a few yards of the shack, half amazed to find that it actually existed. A hodgepodge of wooden planks, cardboard, random strips of metal, and other scraps, it looked like it wouldn't survive the next thunderstorm. But it also looked as if it had been there longer than the three of us had been alive.

We crouched behind some mesquite trees. Cody made fake military signals indicating that we should sit still and wait the old man out. I bit my lip to keep from giggling at how serious he was. Sam took off his shoe and inspected the thorns lodged in the sole.

After what Cody decided was a sufficient amount of time, with no sight of the man, he whispered to me, "You go in."

"Hell no."

"Oh, you fucking punk."

"Fuck you!"

Wide-eyed and frustrated, we cursed each other in hushed tones until we agreed to go in together. I grabbed a tree branch of my own just in case the man was as crazy as we thought. Cody looked at me like I was a wimp for doing so, then grabbed a branch too.

With our weapons raised high above our heads, ready to beat anything that moved, we crept up to the shack. If a rabbit or squirrel had darted out of the tall grass right then, we would have pummeled it out of sheer panic.

Rounding the corner of the shack, though, we found that it was empty, aside from the smell of piss, some candy wrappers, and beer cans. It looked like a hideout for kids a little older than us, not for a wild old man.

"Well, shit," said Sam. "All that for nothing!"

"I knew it was all bullshit," said Cody, even though it was his idea.

I had already turned around and started clambering back through the tall grass when Sam started cursing again.

"Holy fuck! Holy fuck! Holy fucking fuck!"

At first, I thought he was just holding up a pile of tattered newspapers. Taking a step closer, I made out, just under the part of the page he was holding, a topless woman. Head thrown back, rouged mouth open. Sam was holding three rain-soaked magazines.

The word "porn" hadn't even made it out of my mouth before Cody made a run at his brother. He lunged to snatch the magazines out of Sam's hands, but Sam threw himself to the ground, tucking the magazines under his stomach. Cody gave Sam a few good kicks. Sam wasn't budging, though.

"Fuck you," Sam spat while Cody looked at the tree branch in his hand like he was ready to make use of it.

"Stop," I said before I knew what I was doing. "I saw three."

"What?"

"Sam held up three magazines."

Cody stooped down again to turn his brother over, but Sam still wouldn't budge. He had some mud on his chin. "They're mine! I found them! Fuck y'all!"

"God damn it," exhaled Cody. He raised his branch like a hammer and cracked it over his little brother's back. The branch broke in half, and Cody walked off like he was looking for something bigger.

"What if we shared?" I said, keeping an eye on Cody while he tested the weight of another branch. "Sam, there are three, right?"

"Yeah."

"Okay. What if we each got a copy and traded . . . or something?"

Sam put his chin back on the ground and mulled the idea over. Cody had stopped moving behind me.

"I found 'em so I get to choose which magazine I want first," Sam finally said.

"All right." I nodded, turning to Cody. "All right?"

"Yeah," he said, more to the branch he was holding than to us.

Sam made Cody and me keep our distance while he paged through the magazines, deciding which one he wanted. Each of us would have a magazine for two nights, then we would trade.

"Come the fuck on already," Cody yelled.

"Fuck you!"

"Sam . . ." I said, starting to enjoy my role as hostage negotiator.

"All right, I want *Hustler*," he said, then threw us the other two magazines. I took *High Society*, which left Cody with *Playboy*. Each of us shoved our chosen magazines under our shirts — thinking nothing of just how gross that was — and headed back to the apartment complex. We didn't mind the

30

thorns anymore. Instead of cursing, we started chanting different names for porn. When we got to "smut," we liked the way it sounded, and it replaced all other words in our chant. "Smut, smut, smut, smut," we whispered, all the way back to our apartments.

Right where the sidewalk forked, leading to our separate buildings, I patted the magazine under my shirt and said, "Two days."

Cody nodded. "Two days."

"Smut," added Sam.

In the dark, alone in bed with my copy of *High Society,* I eased down under the sheets, but kept the light in my closet on so I could see. Mom was in her bedroom on the other side of the apartment, watching television. Every time I heard her footsteps, I would shove the magazine under my pillow and pretend to be asleep until I was sure it was safe. My heartbeat kept speeding up, then slowing down again.

I flipped through the pages carefully, afraid the magazine might fall apart in my hands. The pages were faded and grainy to the touch. The image of a ragged old man in a shack jacking off to this very magazine surfaced for a moment, then I pushed the vision away. I couldn't shake him, though. My finger brushed against the surface of one of the magazine's rough pages and I thought of skin, wrinkled and uncared for. Had the homeless man been there all along, watching us from the safety of the nearby trees? With his face pressed against the leaves and bark, had he stared out at the three boys stomping into the woods, ready to break already broken men just because it was summer, because boredom was made to be broken, cracked open, and robbed? Where was this man now? Had he returned to his shack to rest? Could he see the stars from where he was sleeping tonight?

Again, I tried to push the thought of him away. There probably hadn't been a man at all. That's what I told myself. I paged through the magazine distractedly, until I came to a spread that began with a wealthy housewife inviting her chauffeur inside for a glass of wine.

I was surprised to find that the magazine spreads were so glamorous. I thought it would just be picture after picture of naked women posing, but this magazine had plot lines. The pictures looked like stills from a soap opera in which every scene builds to the same inevitable conclusion. A wealthy white woman tanning by the swimming pool while the pool boy looks on. A wealthy white woman taking a bath with all her jewelry on while her husband shaves his beard.

The women, and their perfect makeup, and the heels they kept on at all times, became a blur. But one man stood out: the chauffeur. He had green eyes, olive skin, and a body that made me wish I knew words in a foreign language. By luck, the page on which he appeared wasn't faded or ruined by the rain. He kept his black jacket on, but nothing else, reclining on the couch while the housewife kneeled before him. She was posed off to the side, legs impossibly splayed.

There is something about being able to study another man's body. No sneaking glances or peeks, no pretending to be looking at something else. There is something about the unshielded gaze. Once in my middle school PE class, we were all sitting on the gym floor while the coach showed us how to make a perfect free throw shot. He kept aiming for the top right corner of the square and making the shot over and over to prove his point. Tyler, a boy near me, was sitting cross-legged in his soccer shorts. My eyes followed his bare thigh up to where his balls had slipped out of his loose boxer shorts. They were pink and smooth, not quite hairless. I wanted to keep looking — I wanted to really see him — but I forced myself to turn back to Coach, still making one perfect free throw shot after another. For the rest of class, my eyes kept finding their way back to Tyler, then darting away a second later. One more good look, that's all I wanted. And, of course, that's not all I wanted. But it was all I wanted until I had it.

In bed with that dingy copy of *High Society,* I could stare at the naked chauffeur's body full on and for as long as I wanted. Sometimes he was posed as if looking up at me, other times he'd stare into the housewife's eyes, their bodies hooked into each other. They knew they were not alone. In one shot, the housewife had a smirk that reminded me, briefly, of a smiling man I'd seen before. "Caught me again," I imagined her saying, just before going back down.

With the magazine tucked into the front of my shorts, I met Cody and Sam back on the sidewalk between our apartment buildings. After they walked up, I reached to pull out my magazine but Cody held up his hand to stop me.

"Not here. Let's go to our place." He saw the question on my face and added, "Safer."

I don't know what I thought their apartment would look like, but all the doilies, pink lampshades, and porcelain animals threw me off. I guess I thought the apartment would look like Cody and Sam themselves, the décor equivalent of sweat-stained soccer jerseys, faded jeans, and Vans. When I reached to pick up a white porcelain elephant, Cody looked at me like he was going to punch me so I left it alone and followed him into his bedroom.

Sam plopped down on the bunk bed and took his magazine out from under his shirt. "Which one do you want?" he asked, flipping through his copy of *Hustler* one last time. I caught a glimpse of a topless woman arching her back. No pearls and champagne glasses.

"I want the *Playboy*," I said, looking over at Cody. He shrugged and handed it to me. I paged through the magazine and pretended not to be disappointed by the fact that it had so many articles and no naked men at all. Cody pretended not to watch me.

"A lot of words," Cody offered while handing my copy of *High Society* over to his brother in exchange for *Hustler*. "But a few pretty good chicks. I'll say that."

We all fell silent for a moment, flipping

through the pages of our magazines. Since Cody was standing in front of me, my eyes didn't have to stray too far from the pages of my *Playboy* to see the bulge in the front of his shorts, slightly larger than a few moments before. I wanted the answer to the question uncurling there. When I looked back up, Cody was staring at me.

"Ready to go?" he asked, his eyes intense and unreadable, locked on mine.

I shoved the magazine under my shirt and made my way to the front door without another word. Cody's eyes burned holes into my back until I was all the way in the living room. Neither brother bothered to walk me out. I knew the way. Their apartment was laid out just like mine.

When it was time for the next switch, I met them at their front door. Cody opened it but stopped me before I could step inside.

"Out there," he said. Sam smirked.

Backing up, I pretended not to know or care why he didn't want me inside their home. We walked around to the side of the building, over to where the air-conditioning units were concealed by tall bushes.

"Ready," Cody said, reaching for the magazine under his shirt. Sam nodded, his smirk still etched into his pink face.

"I want the *Hustler*," I said, trying to steer the moment back on track.

"All right." He paused, looking at Sam, then me. "Go!"

Cody snatched the *Playboy* from my hands and they bolted, their white T-shirts sudden blurs racing away. I was already sprinting after them before I realized it. With all three magazines, the brothers were making a run for their apartment. At first, I gave chase because I thought they were just messing around, sure to stop any second. But then I realized they were playing for keeps. "Fuckers!" I screamed.

Spotting a plastic baseball bat in the grass, I picked it up without stopping. Just as Cody made it into the doorway of his apartment, with Sam just a few steps behind him, I brought up my arm and swung the bat as hard as I could. The bat struck Sam just above his right ear, but he slid into the apartment and slammed the door shut.

Alone outside now, I swung hard at the locked door. I was soaked in sweat. Laughter trickled out from behind the door. I started swinging the bat wildly, like it was an ax and the door was tinder. Then, just when I was about to exhaust myself, Cody knocked against his side of the door and yelled, "You faggot!"

I slammed the bat against the door and it cracked open, into two useless black halves. I beat the door with my bare hands until my fists stung and went numb. I kept at it even when I heard the brothers laugh once more and walk away from their side of the door. At last, I slid down to the ground. I don't know how long I sat on their doormat, knees against my chest.

You were never going to be one of them, said the lightning in my shoulder. *Stupid, stupid, stupid,* answered the thunder in my fists. I felt like I'd been split open. And my head rang with Cody's voice.

You faggot!

It was almost a relief: someone had finally said it.

3

June 7, 1998
Jasper, Texas

After a long day of work, James Byrd Jr., a black man, accepted a ride home from three white men. Three white supremacists, he realized a moment too late. They beat him, chained him to the back of their truck, and dragged him for more than a mile down a desolate country road. Jasper, where Byrd lived and died, is just a four-hour drive from the living room where my mother and I sat that evening.

Separated by a heavy silence, we watched the local news reporter's mouth twist and morph to find the right shape for the word "dismembered." I don't remember if we turned to each other then, after Mom picked up the remote and hit the power button. I wish I could. I hope we did. I'd like to think that together we were able to name the fear that burrowed into the both of us that humid evening.

I was the kind of boy who collected rocks. A red book of Greek mythology "for children" was always just an arm's reach from my bed, next to a notebook of, well, not poems exactly, just stray phrases I'd jot down when I was tired of repeating them to myself. When I went to bed that night, instead of going to my notebook, I dug through my rock collection until I found my piece of jasper. The polished stone was smooth to the touch and rust red. I saw the image of three boys with three branches in their hands, stomping into the woods. For a moment, I was less than innocent — not terrified, but the possibility of terror itself. For a moment, I was the wolf outside the door. But then I was a black boy in America again, curled fetal in his twin bed, a bloody stone in hand, ears ringing with the rattle of chains. Silent, troubled, and helplessly myself.

Just as some cultures have a hundred words for "snow," there should be a hundred words in our language for all the ways a black boy can lie awake at night.

4

Summer 1999
Memphis, Tennessee

Mom, a single parent working two jobs, would send me to Memphis to stay with my grandmother for the second half of summer each year. Growing boys devour electricity, fully stocked refrigerators, pantries, and patience, and Mom couldn't afford the cost when I was out of school.

During these summer visits, my grandmother took me to Ebenezer Baptist Church every Sunday. She introduced me to people as "Saeed, my grandbaby visiting from Texas." Her friends would lean down with one hand holding up their extravagant church hats and slip me a strawberry hard candy. These ladies would say, "Boy, I knew you before you were a twinkle in your mother's eye" or sometimes just "Boy, I knew you *when.*" I loved hearing that sentence the most.

But the summer I was thirteen, something shifted. My grandmother started going to a new church, one with a fervent evangelical streak. She stopped introducing me as her grandbaby and started saying: "This is my grandson, Saeed. His mother is Buddhist." The first time I heard it, I assumed she was just in a mood, that maybe the heat had taken some of the usual warmth out of her voice. Then I heard it again and again — that same flat, dry tone as if she didn't know or care that such a sentence would electrify the air in any Southern church's sanctuary.

Mom had been practicing Buddhism since her early twenties, well before I was a *when,* so it's difficult to explain why everything changed that summer. Until then, I hadn't thought of their difference in religion as a source of real tension in our family. Mom was Buddhist; my grandmother and uncle were Christians. In Texas, I went to Buddhist meetings with Mom; in Memphis I went to church with my grandmother. The first few times I heard "His mother is Buddhist," I looked at my grandmother out of the corner of my eye, trying to read her. I saw nothing; she was a cipher. I, on the other hand, was all capital letters. Maybe that's how I would've been anyway that summer. Crossed arms, eyes just waiting for another reason to roll, a hand always finding its way to my hip.

Sitting in her living room one evening, my grandmother looked across the room at me and picked up a conversation I didn't realize had been going on.

"Worldly. That's how you're acting now," she announced. Then she went back to reading her Pat Robertson book. The word had sat on her tongue like a drop of acid. "Worldly."

An evangelist preacher was visiting my grandmother's church that summer and gave regular sermons for most of his stay in Memphis. All he ever seemed to talk about was how we — we? — had to save as many people as possible from the fires of hell. The blood of all the loved ones we failed to save would be on our hands come Judgment Day.

Instead of going to church only Sundays as before, my grandmother and I now went three or four days a week. At first, we would stop at my uncle's house on the way to church to pick up my cousins, who also attended the same church. Uncle Albert was a man of God. Sometimes I would watch him talking to his wife and kids and, I swear, I could see him connecting his choices to the exact Bible verses that were guiding him. I admired that sense of purpose — but it also looked, well, a bit exhausting. Even though I liked him, I mostly steered clear of Albert, already knowing that I'd find a way *not* to live up to all those Bible verses.

As the weeks dragged on, I slowly put together that my grandmother and I were the only ones filling the pew, day after day. No uncle, no cousins. The judgment is obvious now. I needed church in a way my cousins did not. *I* was the blood on their hands.

One night after church, I went for a swim in the community pool across the parking lot from my grandmother's apartment. It was dark so there weren't any little kids splashing around. Except for some adults drinking beer over by the patio tables, I had the pool to myself. Mostly, I just held on to the edge of the deep end while stretching out and slowly paddling my legs. It made me feel long. Once the sun set, I turned over onto my back so I could look up at the stars.

When my grandmother first called my name, I thought it was dinnertime. But when she said my full name — first, middle, and last — I pulled myself out of the water in a single movement. She was marching toward the pool from her apartment.

"Sedrick Saeed Jones," she shouted again,

stretching the syllables into something that only my ears could possibly recognize as my name. She was panting when she finally reached the fence. "Get out of that pool and in this house. Now."

The adults drinking on the patio snickered. As I wrapped the towel around my waist and walked toward the gate, my mind spun like the cogs of a mad clock, trying to figure out what I was in trouble for and what I needed to say to get out of it. When I made it to the gate of the pool area, she turned without another word and started marching back toward home as I followed.

I stepped into the apartment and closed the door behind me. When I turned back, she was standing in the hallway with a wrinkled magazine clipping in her trembling fist. I couldn't see it in any detail, but I knew exactly what it was. Before I'd left Lewisville, I had gone through Mom's pile of *Vogue* magazines and cut out every image of shirtless men I could find. My favorite clipping was from a retrospective of iconic Calvin Klein ads that featured a huge shot of Mark Wahlberg against a brick wall in nothing but a baseball cap and white CK underwear. I thought I had been clever, tucking the clippings inside my book of Greek mythology.

"This?" she said, and it was a question I knew better than to answer. "No. No. *No.*" The words came from a deep part of herself. Each more of a bellow than a word. "No. No. No. No."

I watched her ball up the clippings and throw them into the trash. She stomped into the living room, stopped in front of the coffee table, grabbed my hand, and pulled me down to the carpet beside her.

"Worldly. Not in this house. We are praying *now.*"

I knelt beside her, put my wet, wrinkled palms together, and slammed my eyes shut. My head was full of everything but apology.

A couple of summers earlier, I'd had a run-in with my grandmother. In retrospect, it looked like a warning shot. We were walking out of the Southland Mall when she turned to me and told me to stop holding my books "like a girl." I can't remember why I was even carrying a stack of books, but there they were, three slim books pressed against my chest, secured by my crossed arms.

"Well, tell me how boys carry their books," I spat back. And, without turning to look at me or pausing in her stride, my grandmother slapped me across the face with the

46

back of her hand. I remember feeling the air whir between us. The automatic doors ahead of us opened, buzzing with the sudden mix of the mall's air-conditioning and the sticky heat outside. She walked through, then paused on the edge of the sidewalk, waiting for me in the withering sunlight.

I was still standing inside the mall entranceway, my mouth agape, books still pressed against my chest. I'd learned that year how to dip my sentences in sarcasm; I was always talking back. But I had no words at the ready now. I couldn't even sputter.

The slap had been so sudden, so unlike my grandmother, who I tended to think of as being too quiet for her own good. Had I been wrong to think I knew her? What else could explain the stinging on the left side of my face?

I raised a hand, touched my cheek, and smiled faintly — like a lunatic. Realizing that she wasn't going to apologize, and that we could only stand like this for a few seconds longer before people began to stare, I started walking again. The automatic doors opened and I fell in line beside her out in the heat.

The day after she pulled me down to my knees to pray beside her, I made a decision.

Any minute now, my grandmother would be knocking on the door to tell me it was time to get ready for church. The Wednesday night service started at 6:30 and she would want to avoid getting stuck in rush-hour traffic. That's why she was about to wake me up from my nap. I was already awake, but I had turned onto my side, away from the door, hoping she'd think I was still asleep and leave me alone.

A kid at school told me that people breathe slower when they're asleep so I held my breath, trying to control it. The concentration made blood rush to my ears. I could hear my pulse. I could hear everything: robins in the poplar tree outside my window, kids splashing in the pool, my grandmother washing dishes, my grandmother putting the dishes away, my grandmother turning off the TV, my grandmother walking toward the guest bedroom where I was pretending to be asleep.

She opened the door without knocking.

"Saeed, time to get up." There was a slight song in her words. I could feel her standing in the doorway, watching me. She knew I was pretending.

"Saeed. Get up." The song was gone.

Without turning to face her, without taking my eyes off the window, I said, "I'm not going." I had thought this through. "I don't want to go" would sound like whining. "Don't make me go" would sound like begging. I wanted to be taken seriously, so I said the words as slowly and deeply as possible.

She shifted from one foot to the other. I couldn't remember if I had actually spoken out loud or in my head, so I repeated myself. I hoped that for once when I opened my mouth a man's voice came out: "I'm not going."

She walked over to the bed and stood beside me. "Get out of that bed."

I tried my best to say it without my voice cracking, without a hint of a whine:

"No."

In one swift motion, my grandmother grabbed the sheets and yanked them off the bed. It was like a magician removing a tablecloth while keeping the dishes on the table. I turned over to look at her. We both had the same glare in our eyes.

And I knew that it was over. I would go to church. I would sit next to her. We wouldn't look at each other. I would grind my teeth to the sound of the evangelist's voice. I would roll my eyes at my grandmother's prayers.

She watched me scoot out of bed and walk

to the dresser. I put on my clothes in silence. My grandmother didn't leave the room until I had my shoes on.

At the end of the service that night, the preacher stepped out from behind the podium and spread his arms. I didn't see the preacher's smile. I saw the oil on his nose and the beads of sweat on his neck. He always did this. He would stand with his arms spread wide open until someone walked to the front of the room, sobbing audibly.

"Come to the pulpit and let us pray together."

He said it with the same tone he had used for the last few weeks, three nights a week. He tried to sound like this was spontaneous, like he had just been standing there and could suddenly feel us asking for prayer.

I had come to develop an odd fondness for this moment, because it meant that the night was almost over. Soon, my grandmother and I would be driving back home. She caught my eyes. And I noticed that her eyes were shining, like she was about to cry. Her hand was on my hand. She was holding my hand. I thought she was about to lean forward and apologize. I smiled.

She pulled me to my feet. My body felt

hot, then numb. We were moving toward the front of the room. People were craning their necks to watch us as we passed them. People were applauding and saying amen. I tried pulling away, but my grandmother wouldn't let go of my hand.

When we got to the pulpit, the preacher was wiping sweat from his face with a handkerchief. He got on his knees and we did the same, my grandmother pulling me down to the floor. I felt it again then, the same kind of awe that years before made me hold my palm against my stinging cheek. This time, though, it spun itself into a new kind of heat. I could have set that room on fire.

"This is my grandson Saeed. His mother is Buddhist."

The preacher nodded his head like it was all he would ever need to know about me — not that I held my books like a girl, not that I was worldly, not that I collected pictures of naked men the way I used to collect rocks. He started to pray out loud for the entire church to hear. "Dear God, hear me, praying for one of your lambs. His mother has chosen the path of Satan and decided to pull him down too."

I was dizzy. It felt like all the lights in the room were on me. I wondered what my back looked like to the people in the pews. My head was bowed. I probably looked like I was crying. I wanted to turn and scream out that I was not my mother's fault.

"Fight back, God. Make her suffer."

The word "her" hit me. If only I could grab the fire blazing through me and hold on to it long enough to roar back at this man, "Who the *fuck* are you?! I *know* you aren't talking about *my* mother!" But I couldn't do it. I kept my head down, stunned and silent. I felt my knees wobble as if I might fall onto my side.

"Put every ailment, every disease on her until she breaks under the weight of the Holy Spirit."

I turned my head slightly and looked at my grandmother. My mother had a heart condition. When I was five, she had been on the list for a heart transplant. My grandmother knew all of this. She *knew* her daughter's heart. Her head was bowed and her eyes were closed. She was frowning, but I couldn't tell if it was because of me or him. This man was cursing her daughter. Her *daughter.* The body that linked our bodies.

"Show her your plagues and save this child. Amen."

"Amen."

The preacher was finished, and my grandmother quietly thanked him. I couldn't
think of anything to say so I just stared at
her. My mouth was open and my eyes were
wide, bewildered, stinging. She took my
hand and patted it, and slowly rose to her
feet. She had a bit of trouble standing up —
I'll never forget that tiny stumble — so I
helped her regain her footing. For a moment, my grandmother disappeared back
into herself; she was just an old black
woman again, soft-spoken, meek, even.
Then the spell broke. She dug around in
her purse, found her keys, and stepped
down from the pulpit without looking at
me. I watched one person after another pat
her back and shake her hand as she made
her way down the aisle and out of the room.

I don't remember following her. The
memory begins to flicker like a broken film
reel here. It burns itself blank and then we
are in my grandmother's car.

The windows were rolled down because
her AC had been broken all summer. A
breeze drifted into the car, then slipped
away as if it knew to leave us alone. I kept
my eyes on the road ahead of us, yellow line
after yellow line passing while I clung to the
only grace I knew that evening: that the
summer would end, and I would leave

Memphis. That I would never come back, never spend another summer with my grandmother. This fact was as palpable as the silence.

Looking back now, I think she felt it too — the speed with which I was slipping away from her. Perhaps she had felt this all summer long and the church visits had been her last-ditch effort to keep hold of me, her "grandbaby visiting from Texas," who was "worldly" now. I wish I had known that, really, this was always how it was going to play out for the two of us, one way or another. Precisely because my grandmother loved — loves — me, she tightened her grip until it became so painful that I had no choice but to yank myself free.

People don't just happen. We sacrifice former versions of ourselves. We sacrifice the people who dared to raise us. The "I" it seems doesn't exist until we are able to say, "I am no longer yours." My grandmother and I, without knowing it, were faithfully following a script that had already been written for us. A woman raises a boy into a man, loving him so intensely that her commitment finally repulses him.

Silent beside my grandmother on the same twenty-minute drive we'd taken so many times that summer, I could feel the distance growing but didn't understand it yet. Instead, a sense of certainty took root in me.

I made myself a promise: even if it meant becoming a stranger to my loved ones, even if it meant keeping secrets, I would have a life of my own.

Maybe she had been right about me after all. *Worldly:* "concerned with material values or ordinary life rather than a spiritual existence." *Worldly:* "experienced and sophisticated."

Of course I wanted to see the world, to experience its fullness. I wanted to be a real part of it, rather than the passing shadow I so often felt like. I wanted to devour the world.

I sat there ablaze, struggling to apprehend a new, darkly radiant sense of self. I felt dangerous, evil even.

If this feeling was what my grandmother meant, I wasn't sure I would survive it after all.

But I couldn't turn to her now — not anymore — to name whatever was having its way with me. So we drove on, an old woman and her grandson, alone together, making their way through one last gorgeous summer evening in Memphis.

■ ■ ■ ■

PART TWO

■ ■ ■ ■

Somewhere between the fact we know and the anxiety we feel is the reality we live.

— MAMIE ELIZABETH TILL-MOBLEY

Part Two

5

Fall 2001
Lewisville, Texas

You never really forget your first. Where and when and who you were: sixteen years old at the football game, twenty-six outside the bar, twelve on the playground. Or who *they* were: all the boys with mouths shaped like knife wounds, the men in scuffed boots, the ones who looked like your father or brother.

You never forget when the word was first hurled at you, or whether a fist or a baseball bat came swinging right behind it. Whether it was whispered, spat, or graffitied. Whether it was costumed: sissy, punk, queer, pansy. "You like that." "I'm not that way." "I bet you like that shit, don't you?"

You never forget your first "faggot." Because the memory, in its way, makes you. It becomes a spine for the body of anxieties and insecurities that will follow, something to hang all that meat on. Before you were just scrawny; now you're scrawny *because* you're a faggot. Before you were just bookish; now you're bookish *because* you're a faggot.

Soon, bullies won't even have to say the word. Nor will friends, as they start to sit at different lunch tables without explanation. There will already be a voice in your head whispering "faggot" for them.

I still dreamed about Cody every so often, even though I hadn't seen him for two or three years. My dreams usually started with his mouth and the way it must have looked when he said the word. "Faggot" is slick with spit. He's on the other side of that locked door, saying "faggot" over and over again, taking off an item of clothing each time he says it. Cody in a pit-stained wife beater, cargo shorts unzipped and at his ankles, red plaid boxer shorts sliding down his legs, the faint happy trail revealing more and more of itself, the base of his dick, a pale pink root.

Cody — in my mind — became the word itself.

"Faggot" swallowed him whole and spit him back out as a wet dream.

Before him, the first wet dreams that I remember weren't about boys or girls so much. It started with amorphous bodies. A pair of beautiful legs, a chest pressed against the small of my back, a cloud of hot breath on my neck, an improbably long tongue tracing my entire silhouette. The dreams weren't gendered. Shadows would keep the faces out of view. There weren't breasts, but smooth, perfect curves. There weren't dicks, but throbbing veins. That feeling knew no gender, until Cody happened. And, in dream after dream, kept happening. By the time I started high school, the bodies of men seemed, suddenly, almost aggressively present. Not just in my dreams, but all day long. *Men were everywhere. A plague of miraculous bodies.* How had I not noticed before?

Just after I started my sophomore year of high school, a black construction worker spent three days working on the roof of our apartment building. There were other men on the roof each day, but his body is the body I remember: shining with sweat as if he'd been dipped in coconut oil from head to toe, the red tone of his brown skin radiant in the sunlight, muscles straining as he worked on the roof's tiles. And a smile so bright, it was vulgar. Coming home from school, I'd find reasons to hang around, even going so far as to set out a pitcher of ice water for the workers one day. Once, in passing, he called me "youngblood." I repeated it to myself under my breath, trying my best not to smile too obviously while he could see me.

His body became an idea I dragged into bed with me at night. Or I'd pull in the body of my track coach, or one of the football players Mom cheered on while watching *Monday Night Football.* How did other people concentrate with all these bodies just walking around all the time? So many men and boys, each with bodies to study and memorize.

Well into high school, in all these dreams I had the body of a girl. The kind of girl I thought these guys would sleep with. The construction worker's wife, the football player's girlfriend, the woman framed in the photograph the track coach kept on the wall in his office. Any woman would do. Any body but my own.

The rough little poems I had started writing by then were usually in the voices of women and usually overly obsessed with Greek mythology. As Medusa, I wrote about refusing to look at myself in the mirror, lest I turn myself to stone. As Penelope, I wrote about dreaming of my husband's body, years crashing between us like waves. As Eurydice, I wrote a poem in which I mistake the heat of the underworld for the warmth of Orpheus's body curled around my own in sleep. Always poems from mythic women about the distance between their bodies and the bodies of their beloved.

6

Spring 2002
Lewisville, Texas

My English teacher interrupted the beginning of class just as we were taking our seats and digging out our books. In a few minutes, she said, the school's theater department would be performing an abbreviated version of a play called *The Laramie Project*. It would be an all-school assembly and take up most of our class time. Smirks and pleased whispers at that last detail. The teacher raised her voice, reminding us to be mature and thoughtful, but she didn't explain why the reminder was needed.

I knew, though. Hearing my teacher say "Laramie" was like watching a grenade bounce across the floor of our classroom. I tried to read my classmates' faces without changing the bored expression on my own. I did my best to mirror the easy shoulder shrugs and grinning relief I saw around me as we streamed out into the hallway.

The Laramie Project was a series of monologues based on interviews in the weeks after the murder of Matthew Shepard. He was a gay twenty-one-year-old man who'd been brutally killed by two strangers he'd met one night in Laramie, Wyoming. I remembered the moment I'd heard about it, watching the news at home with Mom, only a few months after we had sat on the same couch and watched reports about James Byrd Jr.'s murder. A photograph of Matthew — skinny, blond, smiling — was displayed while the details of the case were discussed. I remember thinking he looked sweet, hopelessly gentle. The kind of kid I'd hang around with after school, but only when people I knew weren't around. Realizing that this was who I'd been for Cody made me wince.

Watching the news, I'd thought I could feel my mother turning to look at me, so I'd gotten up and walked out of the living room as if I were bored. She didn't say anything about it that night. "Gay" was still an unspoken word in the house, an increasingly eloquent, encompassing silence.

By the time Matthew Shepard's life and death made it to the classrooms of my high school in 2002, my feelings about him and

James Byrd Jr. had started to swirl and converge. I was walking through a dusty, fluorescent-lit hallway — halfway to the assembly hall, trying with every filament of my body to look cool — when the two truths finally collided:

Being *black* can get you killed.

Being *gay* can get you killed.

Being a black gay boy is a death wish.

And one day, if you're lucky, your life and death will become some artist's new "project."

As the house lights dimmed, I sighed, relieved to be invisible again. Sitting in the dark just before the stage lit up, I heard or thought I heard a senior in the row ahead of me say something about a "dead gay boy." He turned to his friend, maybe to deliver a punch line, or maybe not. Their backs were to me, so I couldn't tell what they thought about this dead gay boy.

Within just a few minutes, some of the girls on my row were sobbing. A few held one another's hands. The monologues were heart-shattering.

I envied the girls who felt comfortable enough to cry, how easily they breathed. All the boys near me looked indifferent. I would think, later, that maybe some of them were only pretending to be indifferent. Maybe some could only sit comfortably, whisper ironically, laugh audibly, with total effort. For me, it took all I had to sit still and silent. I wanted to be on that stage, speaking the words I still didn't feel safe enough to say on my own.

One of the last monologues the students performed was in the voice of Matthew Shepard's father. He was speaking to the two convicted murderers during their sentencing hearing. Dennis Shepard, an oil industry safety engineer, offered them a stern mercy. Instead of the death penalty, he asked for a life sentence — as Matthew would've wanted, he said. He prayed for the killers — or perhaps cursed them — to think about Shepard every day for the rest of their lives.

The girl sitting right in front of me let her head drop to her chest as if felled. She shook her head back and forth, crying softly. It repulsed me then, her freedom. The actor onstage continued his monologue. As best I could, I pushed the words away while keeping my eyes on him. The spotlight made his tear-filled eyes glimmer and I sat there in the dark, trying to ignore a second girl now sobbing right next to me. I tuned out the words he spoke for fear that if I let myself pay attention I would start crying too. I would start sobbing and not be able to stop, not until long after the houselights came up.

But then the houselights did come up. And I slipped on the forcefully carefree posture of the other boys around me. The existential shrug of young men afraid to admit that they've been touched by art, and that they want to be touched in that way again.

A few weeks later, I came home from debate practice to find Mom sitting in front of the computer. She was smoking a cigarette, staring at the front door as I walked through it. Mom rarely, if ever, smoked inside the apartment. And when she did, she would sit by an open window or go stand on the balcony. Even if I couldn't yet feel her stare laying into the back of my neck as I closed the door behind me, the haze of smoke hanging in the air was proof enough that I'd stepped right into their trap.

Walking over to the desk, I stared at the dark stain her lipstick left on the cigarette, then at the computer screen itself; anything to avoid meeting her eyes. The "Older4Younger" chat room window was on the screen as well as the message she'd written to the last man I'd spoken with. I'd been visiting gay chat rooms for months by then, because I had questions — so many questions — and urges that I decided had gone unanswered long enough.

A few years before, Mom had recorded an episode of *The Oprah Winfrey Show* about "sex education" and left it on the kitchen counter with a note telling me to watch it when I got home from school. It answered the questions I had mostly already figured out on my own, but that only made my other questions more inexplicable and urgent: What about boys who liked boys, what about boys who liked men? Who could we go to with our questions? What about our bodies? What were boys like Matthew Shepard and me supposed to do with ourselves before America had its way with us?

"Read it," she said, standing up. "Before I press Send."

Dear Pervert —
Your profile says that you are in your mid-30s. I'm informing you that you have been communicating ILLEGALLY with my son who is a MINOR. I am his mother. If you ever try to contact him again, I will report you to the police. You are sick. STAY AWAY FROM MY CHILD.

My face burned. "Mom, it's not like *that,*" I said. Or at least tried to say.

She moved so quickly I almost lost my balance. Her face now hovered less than an inch from my own. I could smell the cigarette smoke curling between her lips. Standing nearly forehead to forehead, it was the first time I registered that I was taller than my mother. Some shade of this realization must have flashed across my face, because she locked eyes with me right then and took another step forward, knocking me back onto the computer desk. My butt mashed against the keyboard, adding a jumble of letters to her message.

"Hit Send," she whispered.

I obeyed without a word, jumble and all. Then I slid out from between her and the desk, avoiding her gaze. Kingsley was sitting on the couch, staring at us both. He whined, ever the cocker spaniel, and the interruption seemed to call my mom back to herself. She lit another cigarette and went over to pet him. She had slipped into a new mood, a sudden key change. I waited until she started speaking before I dared move again.

"You're growing up and you have . . . . feelings. Everyone has them; everyone has questions. But, Saeed, *this*" — she pointed her cigarette at the screen — "this is dangerous.

There are men out there who would . . ."
She trailed off, looking at the dog, then at
the living room window as she took another
drag. I could almost see the effort whirling
behind her eyes. The strain of having to
push through the exhaustion of a long
workday only to come home to the job that
didn't pay: raising me. "Did that man —
did any of those men — ask to meet you?"

"*No.* Well, yes — but I knew better. I
mean, my profile said I was eighteen."

She stood up again. "Saeed!"

"I know, I *know.*"

"You think you know."

She let out a puff of smoke, grabbed her
ashtray, then started walking toward her
bedroom as if to announce that she had
persevered as far into this conversation with
me as she could. Kingsley hopped off the
couch and followed her. She waited for him
to make his way into the bedroom then
closed her door.

Only after I was back in my bedroom,
behind my own closed door, did I realize
how much I wished we had kept straining
through that conversation together, how
little I understood of what she had said. Did
she mean that when she was growing up
she had feelings and questions about other
girls and that this was normal? Did she

71

mean all men who were attracted to men were dangerous or only the kind of men I found in that chat room? And even if that were the case, *I* was in that chat room too. I hadn't been tricked or seduced; I had sought those men out. Did that mean I was one of those dangerous men or on my way to becoming one of them?

The older I got, the more frequently my mother and I would push each other to the precipice of what we actually needed to say, only to back off just before either of us was forced to get more specific than vague allusions to "feelings" and "questions." But this only meant that the unanswered questions became ever more loaded.

7

Summer 2002
Lewisville, Texas

I can't picture the face of the first man I tried to kiss. The memory refuses me, just as he did when I lifted myself up from between his legs and brought my teenage body to its full height before him. He looked like he could've been the father of any number of the boys I passed in the hallways every day at school: men who had calluses from gripping footballs and hammers, the ones who sent gravel flying every time their trucks ripped out of parking lots, the ones I tried to study without getting caught staring. And here I was, staring up at him, my mouth just inches from his. I remember noting how neatly his beard framed his lips. The beard itself was well trimmed, in contrast to his faded Texas A&M polo shirt, worn Levi jeans, and work boots. His lips were gently parted in that moment, waiting.

■ ■ ■ ■

Lately, I'd been visiting the library as frequently as ever. I even applied for a part-time job as one of the teens responsible for reshelving books; my application was rejected. Having exhausted what I had decided were all the library's "gay" books, when I visited now, I'd quickly decide on a book or two and then stake out one of the computers with a screen facing away from the librarians' desk. The filters on the computers intended to block out adult content were good, but my persistence made me better. I was in the midst of one of these computer searches when the man in the study carrel next to me leaned over in his chair and looked at my screen as if I weren't sitting there. He turned to look at me.

"Are you into that?" he asked.

His voice was vague, hovering somewhere between curiosity and slight revulsion.

My hand, still on the mouse, double-clicked the exit icon as if without me. The rest of my body couldn't decide how it was going to survive whatever was about to happen.

"What?" was all I could say.

"That," he said again, nodding toward the screen. "Are you into that stuff?"

A sudden and forced stillness. Then, a thin stream of sweat slipping down my back. The heart's pulse whispering in my ear's inner chamber like a coconspirator. *Get up and walk away. He can't hurt you here with all these people around. Walk away, no matter what names he calls you, just keep walking. This is a Saeed-shaped trap.*

"I like stuff like that too," he said, almost sheepishly.

I had started to ease my chair back from the desk. I stopped. A voice in the back of my head spoke, *This is how it goes: a truck pulls up to a gas station and the men inside smile. "Need a lift?" they ask, and James Byrd Jr. considers his answer, while the men inside the truck watch him. This is how it goes: two guys walk into a dive bar and see Matthew Shepard sitting alone. They strike up a conversation, a few more drinks, and then one of them nods toward the front door and the truck waiting in the parking lot. There's room for one more if he wants to join them.*

He stopped looking at me, shifting his gaze out past the study carrel like he was keeping an eye on someone in another part of the library. "You know the restroom out in the lobby, right?" he said.

75

"Yeah."

"Wait a couple of minutes and then meet me in the last stall." He got up and walked toward the lobby without waiting for my answer.

One minute. I could just sit there for another hour until I was sure he had given up on me and then leave. The librarians were just feet away from me. I could tell them a stranger had tried to lure me into the restroom to do unspeakable things. There was a script I could perform; I knew it. Everyone knew this play and its ending.

Two minutes. Cody, the construction worker, the track coach, the senior in the school play, the football quarterback. I'd been looking for this man, or a man like him, for a long time: someone who saw what I saw whenever he looked at the bodies of other men. I couldn't be afraid or innocent, knowing what I knew about myself. I'd been looking for trouble, and I probably deserved whatever happened to me when I finally found it.

Three minutes. I stood up from my chair and walked right through the question hovering in the air between my body and the body waiting for me in that restroom stall: *What exactly did he see when he saw me?*

When he had first walked into the library, greeted by the automatic doors' electric sigh and a blast of cool air, he would not have seen me. He would have had to walk past the circulation desk, the children's books section, and turn at the fiction section, before finally arriving at the four study carrels and computers. Maybe the carrel to the right was the only one available, so he sat there without much thought. Had he then happened to glance at my screen and catch a version of what he himself had been looking for? Or maybe, approaching the carrels, he had hovered behind me, just long enough to see my screen. Had he looked down at the back of my head, trying to picture my face?

I wonder if I looked like a grown man from where he was standing. In reality, I was a lanky, black, obvious teenager, obviously effeminate too, if given an opportunity to move or speak. But from a distance, maybe my body transformed, as the bodies of young black men are wont to do when stared at by white people in this country. Maybe my spine stretched itself into a basketball player's posture, this stranger's gaze giving me something I could never quite seem to give myself: the sense of being a real man, strong, even intimidating.

Or perhaps he saw a black boy's silhouette, a high-school-aged frame, and didn't care, or cared even more. Maybe my exact body — limp wrist, fade haircut, brown skin, and all — was the sum total of the kind of body he had been building with piecemeal stares and stolen glances. Maybe he saw me and sighed, relieved to know that the universe had in fact been paying attention, had responded to his call. Or maybe I was just what was available, a slim picking on the way to the grocery store, in a suburb of some 80,000 people, twenty minutes north of Dallas. A body — no, a mouth.

I walked into the lobby and hesitated for a moment. To the left were the glass doors to the parking lot. On my right was the door to the restroom.

I walked right.

The third and last stall was the only one closed. It opened as soon as I stopped in front of it.

The man stood tall with his hands on his hips, the look on his face written in a language I couldn't read. But I took the boxers and jeans bunched around his knees as an invitation. I tried awkwardly bending forward while still standing, then kneeling on one knee. Then I finally decided to kneel, on both knees as if praying. The floor was cold and unkind. Still standing with his hands on his hips, he merely glanced down a bit as I strained to give him head. It looked easier in the pictures of gay porn I'd been hunting for online. I didn't remember seeing people breaking a sweat in those pictures, but my shirt was already sticking to my lower back. *Focus,* I thought. *Think about how much you've wanted this.* I willed the entirety of my being to my mouth. Beads of sweat dotted my forehead.

I didn't want what we were doing, what he was letting me do to him, to be over; it's just that kneeling on the linoleum tiles stung my knees like a punishment and made me feel so far away from him. So I stood, intending just to angle myself into a more comfortable position. But standing directly in front of him, my mouth just inches from his mouth, lips parted in what looked like the beginning of a question, I realized I had never stood quite this close to another man before. Close enough for the front of my tennis shoes to tap the front of his boots, close enough for the jeans, boxers, and belt he had shimmed down his legs to press against my knees. And what had been starting to feel like work just a moment before was hotly dizzying again: the reality of his body — not another wet dream, or day-dream — right in front of me. It was almost too much, too intense and long delayed and so, just like in all the dreams I'd been dreaming, I leaned in to kiss him.

He yanked his head away, leaving my mouth to grate against the soft sting of his beard.

Embarrassed, I ducked my head down and noticed, for the first time, his gold wedding band.

"I'm not into that," he said. He laughed a bit, as if he were alone and had just remembered an inside joke. Except we were the joke. A fortysomething-year-old man getting an awkward blow job from a sixteen-year-old boy in the restroom stall of the Lewisville Public Library, just a minute's walk from the police department, the courthouse, or the city council office. I kept my eyes on the wall to spare myself from the look on his face. I couldn't bear to watch him transform back into a real man and leave me standing there, still a faggot, someone who swung *that way* and got stuck.

"No, not into *that.*" His Texas drawl worked wonders with the word "that." He was already stooped down, already pulling up his jeans.

However much he was "into that" when I

first crowded myself into the stall, my attempted kiss went too far. In the end, I probably spent more time sitting alone at the desk, trying to decide if I should follow him, than I did in the restroom.

Jeans zipped, belt back in place, he unlatched the door and slid past me out of the stall without another word. I heard the restroom door open and close and then I was just myself again, already becoming a vague memory he could pretend to forget as soon as the electric doors sighed and he stepped out into the sun's glare.

Still in the restroom stall, I sat on the toilet and realized that I couldn't taste him. There'd been so much talk in the chat rooms about the way men tasted; so many hilarious descriptions and names for cum, but all I could taste, swirling my tongue around my mouth, was my mouth. The restroom door opened and I listened as someone walked over to the urinals, unzipped his pants, and started peeing. It was funny, I thought, knowing that just a few feet away from me another man was holding his dick.

I flushed my empty toilet and walked past him toward the sinks. He had on a suit and tie; maybe he worked at the courthouse. After turning the faucet off, I hesitated for a moment as he walked up to the sink next to me. My eyes lingered on him in the mirror just a second too long. He looked up, not at the mirror, but directly at me. I snatched my stare away and walked back out into the lobby. A clerk was talking on her cell, an old man leaned down to sip from the water fountain, the automatic doors slid open for a woman pushing a stroller.

Walking through the parking lot outside the library, even though I knew the man was probably well down the road by then, I tried picturing him sitting behind the wheel of a truck, his wedding ring glinting in the sunlight as he steered himself into traffic. I cut through one parking lot after another on the way home, wondering where he must have gone next. Maybe he was in the produce section of a grocery store now, on to his next errand. He was holding the yellow sticky note his wife had left waiting for him next to his keys. She knew he would forget to pick up tomatoes if he didn't have a list. She knew her man. Or maybe he was just pulling into the driveway in front of his house, letting the truck idle for a few minutes while he sat there, staring at bricks and flagstone, the lawn that needed mowing, a girl's pink bicycle abandoned in the grass.

8

Spring 2004
Lewisville, Texas

When I was ten or eleven years old, my mother had decided that we should take a family vacation to New York City with my grandmother and cousins. I can only remember a few stray moments of the visit, but the city was already wrapping me in its neon grip.

I remember the hotel valet with a maroon hat and suit trimmed with gold, just like in the movies, asking my cousin Alex where we were from. Alex blushed and said, "America." I remember a pink neon "OPEN 24 Hours" sign throbbing across the street from our room's window. I kept waking up throughout the night to check on it, skeptical that a diner could really be open for all twenty-four hours. I remember how shocked I felt when I realized that it had stayed open. Did people sleep here? What were they doing when I was asleep in Lewisville?

I remember struggling to make our way down a crowded sidewalk near Penn Station. My entire focus was on not getting swept away, but Mom squeezed my hand and said, "Did you see that?" She was looking back behind us. I turned but only saw the watercolor blur of the crowd. "Those two men were holding hands," she said. She smiled. I smiled, I hoped at the same thing. But before we had even made it to the end of the block, she squeezed my hand again. "Saeed! There was a man dressed as a woman!"

She smiled brightly but now I felt panicked. I worried that my mother was making fun of me, figuring it had to be some kind of joke or a test. Pretend to see gay men, point them out to Saeed, see if he is happy — maybe a bit *too happy.* My mother had never said anything homophobic, but I'd still never even heard her say the word "gay." In the absence of clarity, my worst anxieties reigned. What could have been a moment of possibility — a glimpse of another way of living, far away from Lewisville — instead felt like a sting.

I didn't realize it at the time but we happened to be in the city during Pride Month. The drag queen, I would think later on, might have been on the way to a gig after leaving the parade. And, somehow, the fact that I hadn't seen her became all the more alluring. This place so coursing and vibrant that wonders would flash past whether you were watching or not. The city's electric hum would stay with me. I knew I had to return to those streets and sidewalks, crowded with people who had found a way to be themselves.

Almost a decade later, I walked through our apartment's front door to find my mother holding a large envelope in her hand. *New York University,* it shouted in purple block text. Mom's eyes were shining. She followed me into the kitchen with Kingsley at her heels as I rushed to rip it open. I locked eyes with her, then pulled out the letter.

Acceptance.

I screamed. She screamed. Kingsley barked and pawed at our legs. She started crying what she would call "the ugly cry," the kind that turns makeup into an inkblot test. I started crying too, surprised at just how relieved I felt. Kingsley got so excited he peed right there on the kitchen tiles. I grabbed paper towels to clean up, as my mother picked the letter off the counter and started reading it herself.

I pretended not to notice that the expression on my mother's face had changed from ecstasy to something far more familiar: quiet, consistent concern.

My financial aid package, the letter said, would be determined separately. It was as important as anything. When the follow-up letter arrived a week later, I got to it first and tore it open. NYU was offering me a loan package that would pay for less than a third of the school's $50,000 a year tuition. I left it open on the kitchen counter beside the pile of bills; I didn't know the numbers on Mom's paychecks, but I knew enough to worry.

I was at her Buddhist altar, chanting, when she got home from work. She watched me from the doorway in her Delta uniform, holding her two purses with her sunglasses in her hand. When she walked over to the counter, I watched her read the letter then walk on into her bedroom without another word or glance toward me. A few minutes later, wearing her housedress now, she walked back into the living room and pulled up a chair alongside me in front of the altar. We didn't know what else to do, and praying alongside each other felt better than crying separately in our rooms.

In the days that followed, my mother and

I slipped into a silence in which we were both well versed. It was the same silence that swirled around us whenever she found gay porn in my bedroom. She would rip it up and leave the shreds in a plastic grocery store bag on the kitchen counter for me to find. I would take the plastic bag out to the trash bin in the parking lot while I took Kingsley for a walk. We wouldn't talk about it.

It was the same silence that rolled into the house like fog when, fed up with her smoking habit, I would throw away her pack of cigarettes or leave a handwritten note on the counter next to her lighter begging her to stop.

In the midst of this particular silence, more packets and forms were arriving from NYU week after week. I was frantically emailing a department head, explaining my "financial situation" and begging for help. In those emails, my own desperation was laid bare. The professor promised to help but eventually hit a brick wall with the financial aid department. She encouraged me to keep trying. Frustrated, I simply stopped responding to her emails.

My mother and I, meanwhile, reviewed every glossy brochure together, cheerily deciding on residence halls and meal plans as if everything was going according to plan. We went on this way as long as we could and when it was no longer tenable, we went on anyway.

Weeks passed, until I walked into the apartment to find Mom sitting in front of the altar, chanting while she sobbed. She turned toward me as I put my backpack down.

"I can't pay for you to go to NYU, Saeed," she said, running her fingers over her jade-colored prayer beads. Just as I had privately been working with that professor to devise a plan, she had been visiting banks about loans, meeting one rejection after another.

"We will figure it out," I said.

Just before the sentence left my mouth, I thought it would sound mature, even comforting. I'd known in some way this conversation was coming. But now, when I finally spoke the words I'd been saying to myself for weeks, they came out as a hollow, dismissive command. The "we" was really "you." My mother's eyes fell to the dirty beige carpet and I retreated to my room.

I thought about all these years we had spent in Lewisville, just me and Mom. When we had first moved to Texas — from Memphis to Dallas — we had driven through Lewisville along the way. It was the summer before I started the second grade, and I remember the matching neon green sunglasses she bought us at a gas station just outside of Memphis. By the time we made it onto I-35, the highway that would take us to our new apartment in Dallas, I'd managed to break my sunglasses. Without a second thought, I grabbed her sunglasses off the dashboard and put them on. She looked at me, in mock disgust, then turned her gaze back toward the road, smiling wryly. The ride felt magical, more like two longtime friends on a road trip than mother and son in search of a new home.

Lewisville has a large water tower next to I-35, emblazoned with the town's high school mascot, Farmer John, and his donkey. Farmer John has on overalls and a maroon shirt. The donkey has steam billowing from its nostrils like dragon smoke. As we drove through on that first trip to Texas, I pointed out the water tower to her — "Home of the Fighting Farmers" in bold maroon letters — and we laughed out loud.

We laughed again, this time at ourselves, three or four years later when we moved out of Dallas and into Lewisville. The joke we'd once passed on the highway had become home. My mother had heard the schools were better here in the suburbs, and her suspicions were quickly proven right. I'd been an honor roll student in the Dallas public school system, bringing home blue ribbons every semester with my report cards. A few weeks into the new school year in Lewisville, my teachers started keeping me after school for tutoring in every subject but English. My mother had moved us to a suburb we could barely afford to live in so I could receive a better education. That hope of eventual *acceptance* was the entire point of us being here. We'd done it — *she'd* done it. And now?

All these years later, Lewisville remained a great suburb for driving through. It didn't have much, but it did have that. There were fields guarded by sunflowers so tall their petals tapped my forehead whenever I stood in front of them. Bluebonnets, the state flower, dotted the meadows farther away from the road, along with Indian paintbrushes, which looked like the stray feathers of some mythic bloodied bird. Racing by in Mom's Ford Escort, AC blasting, radio on full volume, I scream out the lyrics of pop songs I was only brave enough to sing when I was alone.

I would speed down Main Street, which turned into Highway 407 if I drove far enough, and I always drove far enough. I'd head out to where the fields of flowers gave way to empty lots waiting to become construction sites, razed squares of dirt boasting of future homes "starting in the low $200s." I'd drive past subdivisions with names like Mission Oaks, Lantana Estates, and Avalon, where foxes and coyotes wandered the pavement at night, where all the houses still smelled like fresh paint on the inside and were too young to have ghosts of their own. I'd zigzag through neighborhoods that looked nothing like the apartment complex where we lived, homes of red bricks and flagstone that looked happy and normal — not by fact but by contrast — and I hated them and the happy and normal people inside them.

I sped through those subdivisions and down country back roads as fast as the car could handle, then a bit faster. I imagined that I was on my way out of Lewisville, zipping toward a future life, in New York City or anywhere far enough away. In that future, my boyfriend and I could hold hands on the street. We'd stroll through Washington Square Park and smile when a little boy pointed us out to his mother. "Look! Those boys are holding hands," the little boy would say. My boyfriend and I would find a spot in the grass, use our backpacks or each other's bodies as pillows, and read entire paragraphs out loud from worn and yellowed paperbacks.

The rest of my life was waiting for me. *Acceptance.* I just had to get there.

A few weeks later, I got my first sense of what that life might look like. Mom flew to Memphis to visit my grandmother and while she was away, some Buddhist friends of my mother agreed to take me to my first drag show. I can't remember how exactly I brought it up, though two of the women were a couple; I must have felt comfortable enough with them to ask. As we sat down at one of the tables in the small club, waiting for the show to start, one of the women asked, "When did you come out to Carol?"

She read the panic in my eyes and answered her own question. "Oh, she doesn't know?" She giggled, smiling at the other women at the table, and patted my hand. "I just assumed, baby. But don't worry; I'll keep my mouth shut." The other women nodded too and I eased back into my chair.

The only drag queen I'd ever seen was RuPaul, on MTV and VH1. I would stay in my room and dance to "Supermodel (You Better Work)," lip-synching before I knew there was a word to describe what I was doing.

I had no idea how an actual drag show worked. There wasn't a stage, just a clearing in the middle of the tables. The drag queen came out dressed and made up as a carbon copy of Janet Jackson.

My jaw dropped; my eyes went wide. I kept looking at her, then back at my mom's friends, then back at Janet again. Her choreography and bravado were so certain she was almost scary, in the way that being in the same room with someone who is overconfident can make you feel shy. In the middle of one of her numbers, a man walked through the clearing, probably toward the bar. She didn't pause and danced right up to him, pressing her face into his and flipping her hair back and forth so that it slapped his cheeks. He scuttled away. The women at my table howled and then gave me some dollar bills so I could tip my first drag queen. I meekly handed out the dollars and she swooped in, winked at me, and then flew away like a bird of paradise.

Other drag queens performed in the show but they were nothing compared with this Janet Jackson. I thought of them as bland intermissions between the black drag queen's sets. When I said I needed to go to the restroom, one of the women walked me to the door to keep an eye on me. "Just keeping you safe, baby," she added. And I did feel safe. For those women, it may well have just been another night out, but for me it was something more.

That night was the first time in my life I felt like the words "gay" and "alone" weren't synonyms for each other.

I started making excuses to spend time in the Cedar Springs section of Dallas as often as possible. By chance, it happened to be just a few streets over from the Culture Center where my mother and I went regularly for Buddhist meetings. The neighborhood had three or four gay bars in short walking distance, some underwear stores, a leather gear shop, and a bookstore with a café attached to it. I was too young to get into most of the bars except on certain nights, but I'd happily walk up and down the street, looking at the men casually holding hands or reading books in the bookstore I'd have to hide at home if I bought them. The spectacle of *ordinary* gay men baffled me. Just a twenty-minute drive from Lewisville's "Fighting Farmer" water tower, gay men were laughing at café tables, passing a pair of gay and lesbian bars cleverly named

JR's and Sue Ellen's — though I didn't get the reference to the show *Dallas* at the time. Even so, I didn't need to fully understand gay culture in order for it to make me feel welcomed. All I needed to do was look around and see that gay people here didn't appear to be scared, ashamed, hiding, or dying.

During one of my many visits to the bookstore, a handsome older man stood next to me while I was looking at the magazines. I pretended not to notice the tuft of hair at the V of his T-shirt. He took a step closer to my side, his eyes still on the magazines, then tapped my hand. The gesture was so unexpected that I looked at him directly. He nodded toward the front door and started walking.

Unlike the first time I was picked up by a guy, I followed him without hesitation. I remember the sound of the gravel under our feet in the parking lot as he leaned against his truck. He wanted to take me to his house, he said. He lived just a short drive away. I made a hasty calculation: if my future was uncertain, at least I had a present. Despite the risk, I just wanted to go. I climbed into his truck's passenger seat.

Sunlight streamed in through the many windows in his house, making bright columns against the carpet. His home had so much space. Every step I took invited an unwitting comparison to the apartment I lived in. In his bedroom, his bed was so high I actually had to climb onto it.

I sat there waiting for him, pressing my bare legs against the elaborate pattern of his bed's duvet, looking at a framed photograph of this man and his beautiful family. He had a son who looked to be about my age, handsome with an easy smile. I wondered what college he'd be going to in the fall.

In that bright room, holding the photograph so that the bottom of its cold metal frame cooled my stomach, I realized that I'd found my way into one of the happy and normal homes I so often drove by. My body had allowed me to enter.

I found myself wishing the man had a mirror in his bedroom so that I could see — really see — the body that had gotten me here. I had never paid my body much mind. I didn't have the body of an athlete or an outcast. It was just . . . mine. Not the kind of body people praised or remarked upon, really. But now, pressing myself into the bed's many pillows, I felt my body and realized that my body could be a passport or a key, maybe even a weapon. A body like a brick thrown through a sleeping house's window. I got hard then just thinking about all the things I would be able to do with myself.

After finishing his shower, the man stepped back into the bedroom without a towel on and saw me rubbing my chest with one hand while holding the picture frame with the other. With a smile that was almost disturbing in its effectiveness, he pushed me back onto the bed while taking the photograph away from me. He turned it facedown on the nightstand then set upon me like the sunlight itself.

9

May 2004
Lewisville, Texas

I had just gotten into bed when I heard my mother call my name from her side of the apartment. I ignored her.

Every few nights lately, she'd been having nightmares that usually ended in her screaming out my uncle's name in the dark. "Albert," she'd yell with her eyes closed. "Albert," as she tossed and turned on her pillow. She sounded like she was a little girl again, trying to wake up her big brother. But whenever I shook her awake, she'd stare at me without seeing me, her face streaked with tears, then fall back asleep instantly. When I would ask her about these episodes in the morning, she'd have no memory of them.

The second time she said my name this evening, she sounded closer, like she was out of bed. Her voice was strange, somehow soft and raw at once. I jumped out of bed, scaring Kingsley.

I could barely make out her silhouette in the dark living room. The image stunned me into silence. Wearing her black house-dress, she was half crawling, holding on to the back of the couch as she slowly pulled herself toward me.

"Saeed," she rasped, "I can't breathe. Call 911."

I ran to the phone, watching as my mother slid back down to the carpet. She settled into an awkward kneel. The dog, calm for once, sat with her while I spoke to the dispatcher. An ambulance's red and blue lights soon lit up the apartment complex's parking lot.

I put Kingsley back in my bedroom and watched the paramedics give my mother an oxygen mask. They tested her pulse and blood pressure, quickly and calmly. By chance, they had her sitting in the chair facing our altar. Having these two white men in our home, inspecting my rasping mother as she sat in her threadbare housedress, made me feel dizzy. I sat down on the couch to still myself.

Speaking slowly between deep breaths, still winded but more herself, my mother finally spoke. "I collapsed in the parking lot after work today."

Her eyes met mine. She looked like she was ashamed she hadn't told me. I was ashamed I hadn't noticed. As far as I could remember, she had just come home like any other day and gone into her room to watch TV. I glanced at the kitchen counter on the other side of the room: a pack of cigarettes sat right next to her orange pill bottles of heart medication, alongside the piles of bills and the new stack of forms and packets from NYU. My hands clenched into fists.

"I thought it was the heat," she said after pausing to inhale more oxygen. "A security guard found me and took me to my car. I rested for a few minutes, until I got my breath back." She looked at me again. "I really thought it was the heat."

It was as if I were seeing my mother clearly for the first time in weeks. The dark circles under her eyes, the crow's-feet, her chapped lips, her rough, dry hands, and chipped fingernail polish. *Look what you're doing to your mother,* a part of myself whispered. *She's killing herself for you.*

The sons of single mothers inevitably encounter well-meaning family members who like to remind us about our role as "the man of the house." The statement usually made me wince, the way it implicitly merged

100

the roles of son, father, and husband; the way it erased the grown woman to whom the house actually belonged. But standing in our living room, watching her gasp, I realized that the two paramedics were looking at me, as if a question had already been asked and they were patiently waiting for an answer. My mother, hunched forward, resting her elbows on her legs, was also staring up at me. I felt larger than I had any right being, encased in the body of an adult but ignorant of how to use it.

The paramedics said she had stabilized enough to decide on her own if she wanted them to take her to the hospital or if she wanted to drive herself in the morning, but they said this while still looking at me. When my mother met my eyes I knew she was thinking about the prospect of medical bills in light of an ambulance ride. So I spoke up, before she could decide against it, and asked the paramedics to take her to the ER. They helped her onto a stretcher and carried her out of the apartment. I stood on the landing, with Kingsley in my arms, as they loaded her into the ambulance and drove away.

Walking from room to room, getting dressed while also picking up things I thought she'd need at the hospital, I noticed that all the lights were still off in the apartment. Had we been standing in near darkness all this time? Once I had a bag of extra clothes for her as well as her medications, her prayer beads, and her purse, I got in her car. It was quiet enough that as I put my keys in the ignition, I thought I could hear the ambulance's sirens in the distance.

When I pulled into the parking lot outside the hospital, I gathered my mother's belongings and walked toward the nurse's desk. The ER was mostly calm except for a patient screaming in one of the rooms. I raised my voice a bit to say my mother's name over the disturbance and watched the nurse as she typed "Carol Sweet-Jones" into the computer. Just before the nurse turned back to me, the curtains in one of the rooms whooshed open and revealed my mother waving her arms about as she tried to fight off two doctors. She was shouting, drenched in sweat with her hair wild. The patient I'd heard in agony was my mother.

"No, *no!*" she screamed, her voice not her own. "I must win!" Then she raised one fist triumphantly in the air and screamed, "Nam-myoho-renge-kyo" so loudly the other nurses at the station, who until then had been unfazed, actually looked up in shock. The curtains whooshed closed again, sweeping the surreal tableau out of sight. I stood there stunned, staring at the shadows moving behind those curtains until the nurse appeared beside me. I had been standing perfectly still for so long that I realized I should probably move, or do something, anything. But what? My stare slid down the curtain and fell to the floor. It stayed there until the nurse guided me toward a small, sea-foam green waiting room.

Suddenly alone, I felt the images I'd been able to keep at bay start seeping in. If I kept my eyes open, I could still see my mother fighting for her life, her face streaked with tears and sweat, spit leaking down the side of her drugged mouth. If I closed my eyes, I was back on the pulpit in the church, kneeling beside my grandmother. That summer was far enough away for me to pretend I had forgotten about it. The waiting room's humming silence turned into the preacher's voice. "Put every ailment, every disease on her until she breaks under the weight of the Holy Spirit. Show her your plagues and save this child. Amen," he said. "Amen," my grandmother echoed. I never believed that man's prayer had any power, but — all these years later — the possibility that my mother's mother *did* believe in it sapped the air from my lungs.

I realized I hadn't called any of my family members yet. I walked outside, and in the parking lot I tried to catch my breath. I couldn't fall apart tonight too. I counted each exhale until I calmed down, drawing comfort from the heat and the dark. I started dialing my grandmother's phone number but changed my mind before the first ring and called my uncle instead.

When Albert answered, words streamed out of my mouth, monotone and unceasing. I'm not sure I even let him speak. I told him everything, afraid that if I paused, I would realize that I was talking about my mother and not some stranger. "I'll call you back after I talk to the doctors," I said, finally catching my breath. Then: "Can you tell Grandma?"

He was quiet for a moment. I thought about my mother calling out his name in her sleep. "Okay, Saeed. Call me back as soon as you can." He sounded hesitant, maybe a bit disappointed. But I couldn't explain why, in such a crucial moment, my grandmother's voice was not one I wanted to hear.

When they let me see my mother, I noticed her housedress, or what was left of it, had been cut up and put in a Ziploc bag that now rested on the nightstand. She put on that dress almost every day after getting home from work. It was the dress she wore whenever she showed up in my dreams.

"We were just seconds from having to cut open her chest," said the doctor. He said something about congestion, something about her heart. I was still staring at the Ziploc bag. He kept talking, trying to explain the sudden change in my mother between the time she left the apartment and the scene I'd witnessed just twenty minutes later in the ER, but I couldn't hear him. My mother, drugged, barely awake, was talking softly to the nurse at her bedside.

"I can't go back to sleep," she whispered, almost girllike.

"You need to, Ms. Jones. You need to go back to sleep," said the nurse as she brushed a wisp of my mother's hair away from her face. Her tenderness stung me. A stranger was so much better at taking care of my mother than I had been.

"I'm afraid that if I go to sleep I won't wake back up," my mother answered. She looked at me, or maybe just a dream of me, then turned away as she drifted back to sleep. I drove myself back home, curled up in her bed with Kingsley, and slept for a few hours.

She stayed in the hospital for a couple of weeks. Friends of the family went with me to the series of events at school organized to celebrate the graduating senior class. At one ceremony, each senior stood onstage and was given a red rose while a teacher announced what college we would be attending in the fall. When she said my name and then New York University to loud applause, it felt like an indictment.

One morning during debate class, my teacher's phone rang. The director of the speech and debate program at Western Kentucky University wanted me to come audition for a spot on their nationally and internationally competitive team. I had recently qualified for high-school nationals and would be competing in a few weeks. They'd heard about me from some other students who had also graduated from my high school and gone on to compete successfully at WKU. My mother was still in the hospital so I flew to Nashville by myself, using my mother's Delta benefits to cover the cost. One of the team's coaches picked me up at the airport and drove me to the campus.

I flew back to Texas the same afternoon

and drove directly to the hospital. A nurse stopped me in the hallway just outside my mother's room and told me she would be well enough in time to attend my graduation ceremony. The nurse put her hand on my shoulder then and added, "I know it's been hard. You should try to get some rest when you can." I forced a smile and watched her walk away.

"You look tired," my mother said when I walked into her room. Sitting on the edge of her bed, I told her that I had visited WKU and that I had accepted a full scholarship from the school's speech and debate team. Her eyes lit up, a sudden brightness that went out as quickly as a flare. She held my hand and squeezed it faintly, trying to smile, as she closed her eyes and eased back onto her pillow.

Congestive heart failure: that's what the doctor had been trying to tell me. From what I had been reading online, my mother's body wouldn't truly recover so much as bide its time against her heart's inevitable betrayal. For months her chest had been filling up with fluid, and it would always be at risk of doing so again. Her heart was essentially drowning.

Watching her sleep that day, shame set in. I had hoped my good news about the scholarship would cheer her, maybe even heal her in some way, easing the stress of the last month. I'd felt heroic flying home: I had figured out a plan for us and pulled it off. Just to watch it fizzle upon contact with the world. The smallness of the victory only underscored how little I understood.

It was as if I wanted credit for rescuing my mother from a fire that I had set and couldn't put out. I wasn't the man of the house; I was the kid who'd finally lit his first match.

■ ■ ■ ■

PART THREE

■ ■ ■ ■

do you know what it's like to live
someplace that loves you back?
                    — DANEZ SMITH

10

August 2004
Bowling Green, Kentucky

"You *really* want to make an impression, don't you?" Mom said.

I was wearing a blue paisley button-down shirt that had a few thin, almost see-through panels, pin-striped boot-cut khakis, and brown leather Chelsea boots that were so narrow they changed the way I walked.

"I'm about to show these Kentucky bitches how it's done," I said, cocking my knock-off Kenneth Cole sunglasses. Whether she intended to or not, she was the one who taught me that clothing could be armor.

Mom was waiting by the front door in black high heels and a black wrap dress, sunglasses on even though it was overcast outside. *Like the kind of women you'd see in New York,* I thought, then forced myself to forget it as I picked up our suitcases and set

111

them outside the front door. She lowered her shades and looked me over. We were both geared up for the journey ahead.

Dallas–Fort Worth Airport to Hartsfield–Jackson Atlanta Airport to Nashville Airport. An hour's drive north on I-65, crossing the state border from middle Tennessee into Kentucky before passing the fields, farms, subdivisions, and town squares that eventually announce themselves as being part of a town called Bowling Green. Then it's a right turn onto Normal Drive and you can steer yourself into the parking lot in front of Barnes Campbell Hall.

Welcome to Western Kentucky University.

We laughed when we finally found the entrance to campus. The first banner we drove past advertised the school's freshman orientation program, known as the "M. A. S. T. E. R. Plan." The sign happened to be hanging near a brick building that didn't look all that different from a plantation.

"Master, huh?" Mom chuckled before turning at the stoplight. "Good luck, baby." I broke out laughing too, almost giddy. I was just happy to see her smiling again, settling back into her perfect deadpan.

I had almost forgotten what I was wearing until I started carrying both of our suitcases, all filled with my clothes and belongings, up the six flights of stairs toward my dorm room. Mom would either wait in the rental car or make trips to Target while I walked up and down the stairs, passing kids and parents all wisely wearing T-shirts and shorts, speaking with Kentucky and Ohio accents.

By the time I'd hauled everything up to my dorm room, sweat had dyed my shirt a deeper shade of indigo. My aching feet made me wince with every step I took. Mom took one last look at me, scanning me from head to toe with her shades lowered. She smirked again.

"Well," she said, looking up at my dorm. "Don't have sex without a condom."

She hugged me one more time, then got into the rental car without another word. She started to pull away before I could even register whether to laugh, or to chase her down with the thousand questions still on my mind. We did this to one another, shocking each other to distract both of us from an impending ache. It worked, in a sense. I just stood in the empty parking space, noticing that the air was thick with the chatter of cicadas. It hadn't occurred to me how much I would miss her until she was already gone.

Alone in my new room for the first time all

day, I put my sore feet back down and slowly took off my boots. I unbuttoned my ridiculous shirt, prying the cloying fabric from my skin. I peeled off my jeans, balled them up, and threw them into the corner. The damp clothes soaked up dust and cobwebs. I'd need to do something about that dust.

Digging through my suitcases, I put on the first tank top and pair of shorts I could find, then started unpacking my books. When I got to my worn paperback of Michael Cunningham's *The Hours,* I sat down again and turned to the scene where a character walks past the arch in Washington Square Park. Going to my classes at NYU would've meant passing through that park nearly every day.

I didn't just feel far away from the city now, I felt small. I felt estranged. I put the novel down and headed for the door and, I swear, by the time I crossed its threshold, my bare dorm room had played a trick on me.

On the other side of that door was a boy — one who hadn't really spoken or introduced himself to other students all day; one who could've made up any new self he wanted — yet who was somehow the mirror image of the pin-striped and paisleyed

Saeed who'd arrived that morning. He was from Lewisville — *Oh, not Louisville, we say Lewisville . . . it's, uh, it's just north of Dallas . . . haha, I guess . . . I don't know, it's just a suburb, nothing special.* He wasn't quite sure how to explain his being in Kentucky. He didn't have a story yet. He was the speech and debate scholarship student who found himself stuttering for the first time in his life and mangling his hellos. His hands were shoved deep down in his pockets whenever he talked, like if he dug deep enough maybe he'd find his bearings. When a girl who said she was from LaRue County pointed out the twin birthmarks on his shoulders — one darker, one lighter — Saeed offered up an embarrassed smile and a mumbled excuse about cobwebs and needing to find a broom. And if, by chance, you asked him if he thought that girl was hot, he wouldn't give you a clear answer one way or another. He would just rush on to the next sentence and ask where you were from.

It just happened. I met one guy who lived down the hall from me and that guy's roommate and another guy who lived on the floor just below mine and then my roommate — the six-foot-four son of a tobacco farmer who'd never been outside the state of

Kentucky — and I closeted myself again. No one shoved me back in there. Maybe I'd just been standing in the doorway of that dusty closet, tripped, and somehow fell back inside.

It shouldn't have been that easy to unbecome myself. The lies and omissions started to roll off my tongue and I got more confident; I stopped mumbling and stuttering. I began meeting people's eyes, shaking their hands confidently, and introducing a person who I wasn't exactly, all while smiling. It felt good, like the first sip of an ice-cold beer after a long, hot day. I could be this person. I knew exactly how to be him. The kind of man who always feels the need to make it clear he doesn't swing *that way*. Lewisville had raised me well.

There were so many freshman orientation mixers and icebreakers that by the time I strolled up to the cookout hosted by the neighboring all-girls dorm, I already had a sudden crew of very nice, corn-fed bros. Peter from Chicago was planning on doing Rush Week. Bryce from McCracken County was thinking about auditioning to be Big Red, the school's mascot. Steven from Danville knew someone who'd make a run to the liquor store for us. These guys loved basketball. Everyone in Kentucky loved basketball, they said. They wore T-shirts with the sleeves unevenly cut off so you could see their farmer's tans. They all had girlfriends or had left girlfriends back home or were eyeing girls at the cookout who could be fucks but never friends. I'd never thought of myself as "one of the boys." I could've made an educated guess about where these boys would've sat in the cafeteria back at Lewisville High School, a table I wouldn't have been invited to join, but here I was: an alternate version of myself in an alternate future from the one I'd been planning for years.

Our RA persuaded a group of us to do trust falls, despite the fact that most of us had only known one another for a day. We paired up on the lawn in front of the dorm. It was just about dusk. The sun eased itself down behind the hills. Breezes actually felt comforting when they slid past you. We all smelled like fresh-cut grass and barbecue. Fireflies and gnats flitted about. And maybe it shouldn't matter as much as it did, but every time I fell, hands were there to catch me.

I woke up in the top bunk in my dorm room the next morning with my body pressed against the cool, white cinderblock wall next to my bed as if I'd been trying to spoon it in my sleep. The sound of my roommate's heavy snoring dissolved the initial shock of not being in my bedroom back in Lewisville. I climbed down as quietly as I could and tried not to stare at him, sprawled over the edge of his bed. I had never shared a room with another person before. The bed almost seemed to rise and fall in time with his labored breathing. I got dressed and snuck out, as if I'd been an intruder in someone else's room.

Kentucky was green, furiously, vibrantly green. Only now, miles and many landscapes away from home, could I tell how parched Texas was by contrast. Even in spring, our greenest green still looked yellow compared with Kentucky. After just a few minutes of walking around, my eyes clouded and I couldn't stop sneezing. Allergies chased me back into my room. From that morning on, I wouldn't step outside without taking allergy medicine first. Even *breathing* in Kentucky had different rules.

In the food court later that week, I finally met some other kids who'd also gotten speech and debate scholarships and would be competing with me on the team. Debate kids aren't all that different from theater kids, except we're more arrogant, tend to speak faster, and have a habit of constantly trying to outdo one another with stories and arguments. Just as I had code-switched my way into fitting in with the guys days before, I started throwing shade, lacing every other sentence with sarcasm, discussing poems and plays, bragging about my aspirations to make it to New York *eventually.* How many versions of myself I'd perform by week's end was anyone's guess.

We finished our lunch and walked to our next session together. Once seated, I saw my crew of dorm guys on the other side of the auditorium. I waved and they smiled, waving back but staying put. I stayed put too. This self was just a little easier to wear. We were there to learn about peer pressure and the perils of getting too drunk at parties. And maybe it's because all week long I'd been thinking so much about what I wasn't telling people, I couldn't help but notice the gaping absence in the middle of the presentation. Something was very loudly *not* being said.

"You know this is all about that Autry girl, right?" whispered Maggie, one of the speech kids who happened to be from Kentucky. When I shook my head no, she gave me the kind of raised eyebrows that precede not gossip but real news.

Melissa "Katie" Autry, a first-year student from nearby Pellville, Kentucky, went to a fraternity party in May 2003. She met two guys, Stephen Soules and Lucas Goodrum, and eventually snuck them past her dorm's front desk and into her room. At one point in the evening, Autry called a friend who also lived in the building and said she had a guy in her room. The friend would later testify in court that a man got on the phone and said Autry had gotten sick in his truck and he brought her back to make sure she was okay. The friend heard another male voice in the background and the call abruptly ended.

Several days later, Autry died in a hospital. She had been raped, beaten, stabbed, and set on fire using hair spray in her dorm room. Soules eventually received a life sentence. And Goodrum — who apparently had ties to the family who owns the Fortune 500 Dollar General Corporation — was acquitted. The case forced WKU to change its campus security policies, especially regarding guests visiting residence halls.

"It was all over the news here," Maggie added. "You didn't hear about it in Texas?" She sucked her teeth when I shook my head again. Autry wasn't mentioned directly during the one-hour presentation, a testament

120

perhaps to the unique talent Americans have for talking all the way around exactly what needs to be said. I remember the orientation leaders continually emphasizing the perils of binge drinking; I don't remember words like "rape," "sexual assault," or "consent." Katie Autry was a specter between the lines. Her story haunted the room, all of us hearing and not hearing her at the same time.

That night, Maggie and I went to our first college party. The host, Rob, was looking me over from the other side of his house's screen door, dressed in complete Catholic school-boy garb, including knee socks, suspenders, and thick-framed glasses held together in the middle with Scotch tape. He was an upperclassman on the speech team and handsome as a good knife.

"My name is Sebastian," he said in an exaggerated lisp the moment he opened the door. "Can I suck your cock?"

I can't remember what I said in reply. Maybe I just giggled and slid past him with my friends, too embarrassed to admit that he could, in fact, suck whatever part of me he wanted. He pushed his glasses up his nose and dramatically bowed as we stepped into the house.

121

The party's theme was teachers and students. In slacks, tie, and a dress shirt, I guess I was supposed to be a professor, though my costume was hardly inspired. Some students showed up dressed as figures from throughout world history or as specific instructors who'd become notorious on campus for being too lenient, too harsh, or just too weird. The older students on the team hosted the party every year to kick off the fall semester.

My first red Solo cup. My first pour from a plastic bottle of Burnett's vodka. My first dark living room with an iPod hooked up to speakers. My first time hearing Talib Kweli's "Get By." My first time stumbling through the house from one room to the next room until I reached a closed door lit from the other side. I got curious and opened it. Clouds of smoke billowed out; heads turned to regard me as I was already apologizing, already closing the door and backing away when someone said, "Nah, let the kid in." My first time realizing that I was, in fact, the kid. I was new again. I was green again. Whatever anxieties I'd been dragging with me all through high school, all the way from Texas to Kentucky, I didn't have to drag them into this house. It was enough just to show up on the doorstep, my necktie poorly knotted, my slacks wrinkled, my eyes blinking as I stared at Rob. Newbie. Youngblood. Baby boy. My first time having a blunt passed to me and pretending to know how to smoke until someone had to show me how. Yes, that is exactly who I was supposed to be: the kid who couldn't inhale, then inhaled too much, the kid who couldn't stop coughing, the kid whose coughing fit made everyone laugh until they started coughing too.

Another first: the door opened and Rob's tall, slender silhouette filled the frame. "There you are, professor," he said. The older kids — even the straight guys — nodded and smiled knowing smiles. The same way they'd smiled when other guys and girls had paired off and slipped through the smoke back into the house's dark recesses. This didn't have to be a secret. It was okay to be a man who wanted another man. We all had bodies, didn't we? And it felt good. For the first time, it felt completely good to want this. No hurt or shame or shadows were tucked into this want. When Rob sat next to me on the bed, I leaned close enough to smell his cologne, a welcome contrast to boys in the dorm who seemed to prefer Axe body spray.

"May I have a word?" he said, taking my

hand and helping me off the bed. He'd been looking for me. He led me out to a backyard that, in the dark, seemed to go on forever. We climbed onto a huge trampoline and lay on our backs, staring up at the stars as they winked mischievously back down at us. I was drunk and high and I could hear crickets blending in with music drifting out from the house. Rob unzipped my pants and took me into his mouth. I realized a girl was sitting on the edge of the trampoline smoking a cigarette as she watched us. I didn't mind. For the first time in far too long, I knew exactly who and where I wanted to be.

11

Spring 2005
Bowling Green, Kentucky

The dogwood trees on campus blossomed first that spring. The petals looked white if you saw them from a distance, as I did one morning while walking up the hill to class, suddenly caught midstride and unsure why. I crossed the lawn as if breaking some invisible boundary, marching toward one of the trees until I stood close enough to see that the blossoms were actually a ghostly purple.

Stroking the petals with the back of my finger, I remembered. My grandmother used to have a dogwood tree tucked in the corner of her backyard. She had sold that house years before. But wrapped in the dogwood's heady scent now, I remembered playing in her backyard when I was eight or nine. Her tree hadn't been much taller than I was back then. I found the two branches that had held the most blossoms and ripped them from the trunk. The raw wounds were pale green and sticky to the touch.

Carrying the branches behind my back, I high-kicked from one end of the yard to the other, in rhythm with a melody I hummed. Every time I twirled, I was both less myself and more. I wasn't a little black boy playing pretend in his grandmother's backyard in Memphis. No, I was a Vegas showgirl making her grand entrance in front of a packed house. I waved the branches like feathered fans, hiding then revealing my stretched legs and pointed toes, before whirling around to peek over my shoulder, making eye contact with one man in the audience as if a spotlight had landed on him.

When my grandmother called me inside, I threw the branches down with force, as if I could also shove aside the rush of embarrassment taking hold. She stood at the door, her brows furrowed, as I slowly walked toward her.

"Why did you tear down those branches?" she asked as I eased into the kitchen's coolness.

"I needed them for my show," I said, trying to keep my voice calm, even as I raced to come up with an answer to ward off whatever she was going to say next. A few weeks before, she had needed to cut me down after I got tangled in the backyard clothesline while pretending to be a trapeze artist. Every blade of grass had been an audience member witnessing my fall from grace.

My grandmother just sighed and walked back over to the lunch she had prepared for us. We said grace over our plates of baked beans and hot dogs and ate in silence.

My answer had been enough that day. I was young enough, *innocent* enough, not to raise her ire. That had to be it. That had to be why my grandmother had seen me without seeing me that afternoon. Eight years old. If I had been even a couple of years older — sauntering into her kitchen like a Vegas showgirl, delivering the same half-answer — I might've earned a slap instead of a sigh.

As the semester went on, punctuated by road trips to Nashville, late-night rounds of Never Have I Ever, and rooftop smoking sessions where my friends and I opened up to one another, I felt the heady rush of another wave of firsts: the first time I felt comfortable asking a friend if she thought the boy who sat across from us in class was cute, the first time I went to a drag show with friends my age, the first time that cute boy from class took me out for dinner. It was my first real date with a guy my age, my first time dealing with the awkwardness of trying to figure out who should pay for what, who should decide where to go for dessert. My first time waking up next to a man whose name I couldn't remember, my first time feeling embarrassed and thrilled by the hickey on my neck after a night of sloppy kisses, my first time surprising myself with how loudly I moaned when I came. I didn't realize how much I had denied myself, or, rather, how much I had been denied by growing up in a time when being an out teenager in the suburbs of north Texas seemed impossible. Well into high school, I had even avoided talking about pop music because I was afraid of what would happen if my friends realized just how much I loved Whitney, Janet, Mariah, and Brandy.

The ferocity with which I seized upon my newfound sense of freedom occasionally baffled friends and classmates. And sometimes it seemed to grate on them, to push them away. Now and then, I got the sense that it was one thing on campus to be an out gay man and another to be an out gay man who liked to have sex, who wanted to fuck.

"Never have I ever . . ."

"Yep, I've done that."

"Never have I ever . . ."

"Mhmmm."

"Never have I ever . . ."

"I did that today."

"Jesus, Saeed. What the fuck *haven't* you done?"

At times, I was proud of my sluttiness. I liked to think that it was radical, as if the act of fucking another man and then bragging to my friends about it was a form of protest against the shame I'd grown up with, and against the shame I felt silently radiating from the new people in my life. But just as often, I found myself pushed to wonder, by the wide eyes around me, whether something was wrong with me. It wasn't that I didn't feel accepted by my friends; rather, I was beginning to worry that I was being welcomed into the fold in spite of some flaw everyone had already decided to forgive. "What the fuck *haven't* you done?" was the kind of question that shadowed me on my walks back to campus after the hookups I was learning not to talk about with friends. It followed me into the shower where, just as often as not, I'd feel like I was trying to scrub away much more than the smell of sex.

It was as if I'd tripped into a gap between the floorboards: none of my friends on campus were willing to talk, but neither was anyone back home.

"I still haven't come out to my mom," I'd occasionally remind my friends.

"Wait, really?" one of them might say.

"I just kind of assumed . . . ," someone else might respond on a van ride back to Bowling Green from a speech tournament.

"Assumed what?"

"I don't know. That you've just always been this way."

Mom and I would call each other once a week, sometimes more. If I managed to let more than a week lapse, I just felt vaguely off and unsure why, until I realized that I hadn't heard her voice in however many days. That's what people in our family liked to say: "I just wanted to hear your voice." We'd say it once at the beginning of the call, and then again at the end — "Well, it was good to hear your voice" — as a signal we were ready to get off the phone. We didn't talk about anything important during these calls, really. The further I went into my studies, the more sensitive I became to surpassing the extent of my mother's own college experience. I thought I risked embarrassing her by accidentally referring to an author or term she hadn't heard of, so I steered conversations away from my studies, except to say that I was doing well. But focusing on life outside the classroom meant having to navigate leading questions about my dating life. When she went this far, I quickly shout-stuttered, "Well, it was good to hear your voice," and ended the call.

When I tried to imagine the conversation I would need to have with her in order to come out, it was like watching a melodramatic silent film without the captions. I cried whenever I thought about it. She *had* to know already. Even with our gift for stalwart denial, there was just too much evidence for her to ignore the fact that her son was clearly attracted to other men. Coming out to her, then, became such a daunting prospect because I knew I would have to lie in order to tell the truth. I wasn't innocent, a naïve boy admitting that he had been wrestling with complicated feelings he didn't really understand. My feelings were clear as daylight. I had passed the moment when I could've innocently confessed myself out into the open.

I talked myself in circles trying to find the perfect phrasing, before I realized there was no way around it. I called home one day while walking up the hill to class. I stared at the mimosa trees while my mother and I chatted aimlessly, until the word "gay" finally dropped out of my mouth.

She was quiet for a moment then asked me to repeat myself. I had started with a joke that my friends on the speech team had been saying about me: *Not even his clothes are in the closet anymore.*

"What does that mean?" she said.

"I'm not in the closet anymore, just like . . . my clothes aren't in the closet." More silence. "You know, because my closet is really messy?" Silence. "I'm gay."

"Have you had an experience?" she asked.

"A what?"

"An experience?"

"Are you talking about sex?"

"Have you had an experience, Saeed?"

"Mom" — I laughed, both embarrassed and frustrated — "are you always going to call it that?"

"Saeed."

"Yes! Yes. I've had — I've had experiences. I'm gay. I know. . . ."

"Do you use protection?"

"Yes."

"Okay," she said finally.

"Okay?"

"I've got to go, Saeed. I'll talk to you later."

After weeks of rehearsing all the possible iterations of this conversation, it had finally happened, and my answers — I guess — had been enough. I'd been able to say exactly what I needed to say without having to tell a single lie, or exaggerate or diminish myself. I'd ambushed my mother over the phone and she had ambushed me in return. Her questions might have been blunt and awkward, but they were without judgment.

My mother called me back before sundown. I had started to worry, feeling worse and worse for blurting myself out to her rather than finding a more proper setting for the conversation. I was at Rob's house with other speech kids, trying to get as drunk as possible as quickly as possible on cheap sangria.

When her name showed up on my phone, I inhaled dramatically and walked out to the back porch.

"I forgot to say that I love you," she said, almost frantically, like she was racing to catch the comet's tail end of our previous conversation. For a moment, it felt like we were both catching our breath.

"I love you, Saeed," she said. "And hon-

133

estly, you sound happy. If you're happy, I'm happy."

After I hung up, her words seemed to hang in the air, hovering amid the fireflies. I stayed out on the porch, drinking the sangria, watching the evening shadows eat away at the light.

I was happy, but the moment didn't feel like I thought it would. It wasn't final. It dissipated just as the dusk did, just as the fireflies fled.

In retrospect, I think I didn't feel as if a burden had been lifted because my being gay was never actually the burden. There was still so much I hadn't told my mother, so much I knew that I would probably never tell her. I had come out to my mother as a gay man, but within minutes, I realized I had not come out to her as myself.

12

Spring 2006
Bowling Green, Kentucky

When the Botanist opened his door, the easy smile I had practiced during my walk to his house flatlined. The picture on his profile must have been a year old, maybe two. The "bored 30-something" who worked out "3× a week AT LEAST" and was "straight-acting and only into other STRAIGHT-acting MEN" was not the man standing in front of me. He'd even lied about the color of his eyes. His blue eyes were in fact brown like mine.

While I stood there, in the elastic few seconds that stretch to contain two strangers meeting for the first time, as they decide whether they want to enter each other's bodies, I didn't think about my own body: more lithe and sinewy than his, not because I had worked to craft this body, but simply because I was young. I didn't think about how I hadn't worked to earn my better body. I just scanned him from head to toe in a single, condescending glance and determined that he had a body that *would do,* a body I could *work with,* a body I wouldn't *push out of bed.*

But if this was going to work, I couldn't go in there alone. I needed to take a memory into his house with me. When he asked my name, I said, "Cody."

The Botanist's head tilted slowly into a nod, as he decided my lie was one he could live with, or at least sleep with. He stepped aside to let me into his house. As I walked past him, I felt his stare glide from the back of my head down to my ass and on down to my calves. When I stopped suddenly and turned around just so I could catch him staring at my feet, he straightened his posture and smiled. We were circling each other.

By now, I knew the ins and outs of names that were not mine and how to wear them like bodies. Every time I met a man for sex, a new name blossomed in my mouth like a flower I could pull out from between my parted lips and hand to the stranger standing in front of me. The names made me into whoever I needed to be for them.

Everyone has a lie we're quietly waiting to

believe. Sometimes we just need someone to show up at our door, keep quiet, and let us do the talking. I gave one-word answers. I nodded and shook my head in reply whenever possible. I shrugged my shoulders in response to more elaborate questions. I made sure my facial expressions hovered vaguely between *interested but not overeager* and *reluctant but not scared.* Together, these nuances allowed me to think of myself as an FM radio that, if dialed just so, could go from white noise to the particular song this man had been waiting to hear all night long.

Maybe a rap song would come on and I'd become a college athlete, a track runner who had a girlfriend and didn't really know what he was doing here but liked it anyway. Or a song by Otis Redding and I would become a preacher's son looking to break some rules before going back home to repent. Or some sad country song and I'd become the guy the Botanist knew in high school and still fantasized about now and then. I could hear the man I was pretending to be as he spoke in a slight Kentucky drawl. *I'm married now with two little girls and a boy on the way, finally. Got a picture of his sonogram right here in my wallet. The doctor even showed me where his pecker is. Said I should be proud. I stopped over to have a beer, catch*

*up on good times. And, you know, well . . . I
don't really know how to say this, but — shit,
I'm blushing like a — Listen, I wanted to tell
you this years ago. . . .*

When I met men like the Botanist, I said
"Huh?" and "What?" more often than
usual, leading them to find me a bit dumb
— which was fine. In my mind, there was a
thread connecting "dumb" to "more manly."
But the real reason I said "Huh?" so much
during these hookups is that I was listening
to what the man I wanted to be was whispering in my head.

The Botanist had the potted trees installed
throughout his apartment. Huge, waxy-
leafed tropical trees were grouped in every
corner of the living room, and in between
were clusters of oddly placed statuettes. It
was like he'd decided to re-create a statue
garden inside his home. The kind of stone
lion you might expect to see guarding the
gate to a large mansion was instead sitting
beside his coffee table. Christmas orna-
ments were hanging from his Tiffany lamps.
It was almost beautiful, this space, just a
few blocks down the hill from campus. I
probably passed the apartment twice a week
and never would have guessed there was a
jungle in 2B.

Still, though, Cody couldn't be interested in something as feminine as flora. I picked up a magazine that was leaning against the stone lion's stomach. The Botanist never sat still for long, constantly finding statues to nudge one inch to the left and picture frames to adjust ever so slightly. It didn't help, I'm sure, that Cody hadn't said a word beyond his first name. The Botanist walked over to a set of glass decanters and fixed himself a drink. When he was walking back to the couch, he realized that he had forgotten to ask me if I would like one as well.

"Oh, I'm sorry. How rude of me. Would you like a cocktail?" he asked, his hip resting against the side of the couch while he looked down at me.

I hated the way he enunciated the word "cocktail" into an obvious joke, and the way he held his martini glass like we were in a penthouse apartment in New York City and not a jungle-themed two-bedroom walk-up in Bowling Green, Kentucky. Cody nodded without looking up from the magazine. Out of the corner of my eye, I watched him struggle to interpret whether that meant whiskey neat or vodka cranberry. I leaned back on the couch, absentmindedly rested my hand on my dick, and watched as the Botanist poured me a Jack and Coke I

139

didn't actually want.

After he handed me my drink, he plopped down beside me on the couch and put his arm around my shoulder, like a high-school jock trying to be cool with his new girl-friend. Cody wasn't into that kind of move, so I scooted away from him.

"So," he said, picking up a conversation that had never really started, "you're a student?"

"Yeah."

He nodded, waiting for me to say more. I gave him nothing; the restraint and forced reticence were turning me on.

"Athlete?"

"Yeah."

I decided to change pace, so I took a break from the magazine long enough to take a swig of the drink and noticeably appraise his body again with a cold look. I didn't want him to think I was shy so much as looking to be persuaded. In order for me to get what I needed out of this night, he needed to want Cody more than Cody wanted him. That, I realized, was why I was sitting on this stranger's couch. I wanted a man to ache for me.

"I figured you were an athlete," he perse-vered. "Those legs of yours. Track team, right?" He stroked my thigh, his hand gliding between my knee and groin. I made myself stay easy and still.

Taking another swig, I spread my legs just wide enough and reclined so I was staring up at the ceiling. The Botanist actually licked his lips.

"Did you find something you like?" My first complete sentence of the night.

He nodded, too eagerly, and pressed his face into my lap. He inhaled deeply, giving me a squeeze with his hand, then sat back up to face me.

"I bet you see a lot of guys' dicks when you're in the locker room. Bet they're not as big as you, though."

The Botanist watched too much porn. That sentence was right out of a scene from a '90s Falcon video. I knew because I watched too much porn.

I took his hand and put it back on my lap.

When he leaned in to kiss me, I could smell his cologne and so I turned away, forcing him to kiss my neck instead.

Yes, I thought about the man who turned away when I went to kiss him in the men's restroom back in high school. I remembered the abrupt sting of his stubble, and the more permanent sting too. But there were rules. You put on cologne for dates, not for what we were about to do. And anyway, it turned

141

me on, just like the forced silence: being somehow unavailable even when I was in another man's hands.

I stood up then and started walking toward his bedroom. The fact that the Botanist let me lead him through his own house, even though it was my first time there, told me everything I needed to know.

The porn playing on his small television cast his bedroom in a blue tint that made us both look slightly more attractive than we were. The blue hit my brown skin and highlighted Cody's bones and sinews. The blue gave the Botanist the body he had promised me.

The TV's volume was turned down low but the video was already playing, which meant that it'd been playing since I first got to the apartment. The bedroom and its blue-lit trees — yes, there were trees here too — had been patiently waiting for us. Three condoms and a bottle of lube were on the nightstand. There were even some tea candles lit.

I shoved the Botanist backward onto the bed and started to peel off my T-shirt. Instead of staying put, he got back up. I wasn't trying to put on a show exactly, but I wasn't rushing either. He decided to help me. With my arms awkwardly above my head and the shirt covering my face, he tugged too hard and the fabric gave a small rip.

Taking another step away from him, I threw the shirt to the floor and sneered. The television's blue tint lit up his eyes and all he could see, standing there in the half-dark, was Cody. I had disappeared right there in front of myself.

The Botanist climbed onto the middle of the bed and got on all fours. He looked back at Cody and growled, "Come on, man!" with a sudden bass in his voice.

I hesitated for the first time all night.

"Let's do this!" he shouted, slamming his hands down on the mattress for emphasis.

I climbed onto the bed, thinking about how quickly our lies can get away from us. This naked, barking man wanted Cody more than I did. The Botanist took over, shouting about how he wanted me to *wreck* him, to *gut* him, to *breed* him. I shoved into him with a thrust that made him arch his back with a loud gasp.

I thought Cody and I had proven our point. But the Botanist shouted, "Come on." He was even louder now, as he backed into me. I didn't like the way he was fucking me even though I was fucking him.

Pulling up my hips, so his back was right

against my chest, I wrapped my arms around him and started to put one hand over his mouth. I could feel the words rising in his throat and wanted to dam the breach before —

"Come on!" he shouted, his spit coating my hand. He shook his mouth free of my grip. "Fuck me with that big black dick!"

That sentence had been in his head since he first saw my profile online. The words flickered when he first opened his door to me, flickered again when I spread my legs on his couch, again when my ripped shirt fell to his bedroom floor.

In that blue-lit bedroom, my black dick was all I was. I couldn't even be Cody anymore. That sentence, screamed out by a white man on all fours, was bigger than me and Cody combined. And I was still inside him.

"Yeah," he growled, "you like that white bitch ass, don't you?" The water is always deeper than it looks. "You like it! That nigger dick likes it!"

As I write, I want to pull myself out of him and out of that room. But outside the Botanist's bedroom is the Latino man who, years later, will look back at me while I fuck him — not hard enough, apparently — and

144

sneer, "Aren't you a black man?" Outside of that bedroom is the dating profile of a handsome twentysomething living in Brooklyn who notes in all capital letters "Not interested in Black, Mexican, or Asian cuisine." Then there is the younger black gay friend who will confess that someone told him once "I just don't find black men beautiful, but I love you as friends." I still don't know what to say to the men outside the Botanist's bedroom. There are so many of them, so many rooms where they are waiting to wound one another with their bodies and their *preferences.* However many masks we invent and deploy, in the end, we cannot control what other people see when they look at us. Lower your voice, change your posture, call yourself Cody, dress differently if you want. A man might still decide that when he looks at you, all he sees is a nigger, a faggot, or both.

I flipped the Botanist over, clamped one hand over his mouth, and kept thrusting. Even when he bit my palm and I back-handed him, he moaned, then laughed, looking up at me with wild eyes as a red handprint bloomed on his cheek. I kept my eyes on the tree beside the bed, which shook in rhythm with our bodies, each waxy leaf shifting in the blue light.

"Harder," he shouted, "harder, harder." And I went harder, realizing that I wanted to use my body to ruin his body. I wanted to be the black savage he saw when he looked up at me; at least then I could make use of myself. I grunted, shoving myself into him again and again. *Fucking bitch. You like that, don't you?* I thought the words were coming from one of the porn actors on the television, but the video was playing on mute and my throat was raw.

"You whore," I shouted right into his ear. "You deserve this."

I tried to fuck my hurt into him, but he just writhed beneath me, moaning that it felt "so good." I wondered how many black men had been in this bed surrounded by trees; I wondered if he had made this jungle just for us.

We came within seconds of each other and I fell onto him, exhausted, spent, used, disgusted by the body right under me. I slammed my open palms onto his back as hard as possible, making him cry out as I raised myself off him.

Standing up, I put on my ripped shirt and the rest of my clothes without another word. I didn't ask to use his bathroom. There was a mirror in there, of course, and I didn't want to see my reflection locked inside this man's glass. My body was shining with sweat, his and mine, but I would have to wait until I was back in my dorm to take a shower.

At the front door, I stopped to look at this man I knew I would never see again. The forest in his living room was candlelit behind him.

"Delete my number," I spat.

He let out a sharp laugh, running his hand down the front of the silk robe he had put on. He locked the door as if I were an unwanted guest finally being kicked out.

13

I went back to Lewisville for the summer to help Mom pack up the apartment. She was moving into a one-bedroom apartment in Atlanta, where she'd lived in her twenties before becoming pregnant with me. This move felt like a circle completing itself; a single mother had gotten her son into college on a full scholarship and now she was moving back to one of her favorite cities as a single woman. To say that my mother was still beautiful would mean overlooking the fact that she'd actually become more beautiful with age. Most people don't survive being pretty; it never lasts quite long enough. But my mother somehow had made it through to the other side of "pretty" and sauntered right into "elegant."

"You're gonna meet a man in Atlanta," I

said, only half teasing her, while I taped up a box.

"All right, you," she replied, her version of "that's enough now." It was what she said when she agreed with my jokes but wanted to at least pretend to tell me to stop. She grabbed the tape and stooped over another box.

"Just make sure he's okay with having a gay stepson," I said. I was still mostly joking, and there was a laugh in my throat that I was ready to share with her. She coughed then went silent. I stood up from where I'd been crouching and watched her rip a length of tape, smooth it down, and move on to the boxes in her room as though she hadn't heard me.

"We've got to pick up the U-Haul before the place closes for the day," she shouted from the safety of distance. "Maybe we should go now."

Just over a year since I'd come out to my mother, it was like that hard-earned conversation hadn't happened at all. We both slid back into the hazy silence we'd inhabited before I went to college. Maybe I was pushing her too far, I wondered. People need time and parents are certainly people, right? Still, I wanted — needed — to find a way to tell her that I was . . . I didn't even know where to begin. Maybe it was best that she kept avoiding me. I grabbed the keys off the kitchen counter, put Kingsley on his leash, and waited for Mom to meet us out by the car.

She started coughing just as we loaded the last of the boxes onto the truck. Or maybe she had been coughing earlier in the evening and I had ignored her until I coughed a few times myself. Moving out of your longtime home means quite literally unsettling the dust of your past. Dust shimmers in the air, coloring rays of sunshine as they cut through the windows. Dust marks the outlines of where your childhood bed used to be. Dust collects in your hair. Your body unwittingly inhales your past and rejects it. As I watched my mother and waited for her to recover, I kept myself busy fussing over details about the move, hoping each cough would be the last. The end didn't come. Around midnight, she struggled to stand up from the one chair we had left in the apartment.

"I'm going," she said softly, "to the ER." I was already walking toward the car keys on the counter. "No, you stay."

"Mom."

"You rest," she said. "I'll go and come back." We had to be at the new apartment complex the next day before the rental office closed at 7 p.m. or we'd be stranded for the night. She was going to drive the U-Haul and I was going to follow behind in the car with Kingsley. But when were we going to leave now? Would she even be able to sleep first?

She took the car keys from my hand and walked out of our dusty, empty home. I curled up with Kingsley, on the floor of what had once been my bedroom, and lay awake.

Being the child of a parent with a heart condition meant living with a paradox. My mother looked and acted fine. Her heart, generally, had no bearing on her daily life. Sure, there were orange pill bottles all over the apartment, but the presence of those drugs paled in comparison to how forcefully she insisted on being herself. So, I had a mother who was sick but didn't appear to be. The fact that I spent most of my time away from her now, talking on the phone or texting, only further reinforced the illusion.

In that way, we were just like each other. We both allowed too deep of a contrast between our interiors and our exteriors. We both clung to self-assured masks that actually allowed us to cause ourselves more unseen harm. My mother hadn't even quit smoking. She had tried several times, of course. But cigarettes had crept back into her routine — my mother's unspoken response to stress and depression. The first time she went out to the balcony to smoke when I got home for the summer, we both pretended not to notice her eyes were bright with tears when she came back inside.

And me. I couldn't even summon the nerve to talk to her about any of the guys I'd dated or how much I secretly loathed myself, much less talk to her about men like the Botanist. A candid conversation about her health was difficult to even imagine.

She woke me up around 4 a.m., only explaining the hospital visit by holding up a white paper bag of new inhalers and drugs before walking out of the room. Still half asleep, I got behind the wheel of the car while Kingsley fell back asleep in the passenger seat. Mom started the U-Haul and led us out of the parking lot.

For the first hour of the drive, the sun wasn't out yet so there was nothing for me to look at but the darkness and the slightly swerving truck ahead of me. Reasoning that Mom was just as tired as I was, if not more so, and the roads were all but empty, I decided I wouldn't call her on my cell until she veered across the white road lines. Then she did.

"Saeed, I'm fine, damn it," she barked on the phone as soon as she answered. "We've got to go." We had pulled to a stop on the edge of the highway, somewhere near the border of Louisiana.

"You're swerving in a huge truck, Mom. It's scary to watch," I said. I tried to sound as calm as possible. "Maybe we should take a short break."

She hung up and started her truck without another word.

It started pouring the moment we made it to Louisiana. The rain fluctuated between spitting, as my mom would call it, and thundering down in sheets so heavy Kingsley would start barking and try to sit in my lap while I drove. The weather relented only when we'd made it through to the other side of the state. In Mississippi, near a town named Meridian, we passed through a spot on the highway where trees leaned over both sides of the road to make a perfect bright, green tunnel for nearly half a mile. I didn't realize I was crying until we reached the end of the trees and the bright sunlight dried the tears streaking my face. The car's air-conditioning went out just past the state border. I rolled down all the windows, made a sympathetic face at Kingsley, and drove on. We took more breaks in Alabama, where I noticed that black-and white-owned gas stations seemed to alternate along the highway one exit at a time. In Georgia, it seemed that every stretch of highway was under construction and clogged with traffic.

After eleven hours of driving, we sat on the floor of Mom's new apartment, eating Chinese food while Kingsley ran from one empty room to the next. Mom had already found the day's copies of *USA Today* and the *Atlanta Journal-Constitution* to read. She mentioned a story about the war in Iraq and I brought up an ex-boyfriend's brother. Any excuse, I figured, to try to get to a conversation with her about all the questions I had — about dating and guys and why it felt like I'd already done everything wrong, before I'd even known what I was doing.

"You know, I dated a guy who has a brother serving over there. Or was; he injured his knee when an IED exploded near his truck." Silence. With my eyes fixated on my plastic container of orange chicken, I kept going. "He's okay, I think. He's recovering in California but wants to go back soon."

When I looked up, she was staring at me, wide-eyed, almost pleadingly — as if I'd led

154

someone afraid of heights to the edge of a rusting bridge. And then I did exactly what I thought all people who love each other do: I changed the subject; I changed myself; I erased everything I had just said; I erased myself so I could be her son again.

At the end of the summer, I made an excuse about needing to be back on campus early to help with orientation for the new speech and debate team members. The truth, of course, is that living in a one-bedroom apartment with my mother, our dog, and all that was still left unsaid was exhausting. I went back to Kentucky and threw myself into the rhythm of what college life had become: poetry workshops in the morning, afternoons practicing for speech and debate tournaments, reading in the library before dinner, then finding a guy to fuck and forget in the same night, or to fall in love with that week, or to "date" that month.

Every man's body reminded me of another man's body. Some guys I slept with just because they resembled a man I wanted but couldn't sleep with. I hooked up with a frat boy just so I'd have an excuse to see the inside of a frat house. I dated a British college student long distance because he said he loved me within the first two weeks of knowing me and because I liked hearing him speak in Welsh on the phone. I fell in love with a straight friend. We wrestled on the bed in my dorm room; he let me suck him off after parties. Then he got a girlfriend and I wasn't in love anymore, just incredibly sad, so I started having sex with another straight boy instead. I dated a guy who went to school in Virginia — my friends called him Robot — because I wanted to prove to myself that I could be normal and boring like everyone else. On a charter bus headed to a debate tournament in Florida, I broke up with him on the phone for reasons I can't even remember. The guys, the boys, the lovers, the men, this one and that one, oh and that one too. Everyone became someone else. And I wasn't green anymore. I wasn't new. I wasn't ashamed of my sex life, exactly, but this didn't feel like enlightenment either. Sex was simply what I did between classes or debate practice to get by, or at least buy some time. I buried myself in the bodies of other men so I could feel something other than the depression that was rolling in like a fog bank.

If I wasn't in class or a stranger's bed, I'd pack a lunch and go to the deepest reaches of the library stacks, weaving through one room after another until it seemed I was the only person around. I'd stay down there for hours, reading poetry collections, eating, taking naps, reading some more, before I had to go back to class or practice. My favorite room in the stacks had one tiny square window revealing people's shoes as they unwittingly walked by. It felt good to be a secret, waiting to be unearthed.

I had mostly excellent grades. I called home once a week, and texted with Mom at least once a day. By this point, I had won several national championships for speech. I was thriving in my first few creative writing workshops. My regular trips to the library meant that when I said I'd read Lucille Clifton's work, I didn't mean just a few poems; I'd read every single volume available. If the university president happened to pass me while walking across campus, he greeted me by name. To all appearances, I was the sunny, shining model of a college student. I'd contorted myself into the image of the young man I hoped my mother saw when she looked at me.

None of this had any bearing, though, on how I felt when I was alone. Standing in front of the mirror, my reflection and I were like rival animals, just moments away from tearing each other limb from limb.

And on days when even hiding in the

stacks didn't work, I'd go back to the Botanist. I'd told him to delete my number, but I hadn't deleted his. Given his lack of surprise the first time I texted him about hooking up again, I guess he'd expected this from the moment I stormed out of his house. Maybe, a decade older than I was, he knew what I would eventually learn: it's possible for two men to become addicted to the damage they do to each other.

I'd fuck him roughly, almost brutally, taunting him until he'd lash out and finally scream racist slurs, which sent me into a vicious loop, my worst fears about myself echoing back to me in a white man's voice. It wasn't enough to hate myself; I wanted to *hear* it. On all fours with this awful man was the only way I could sever the divide between how wrecked I felt on the inside and how put together and dependable I appeared.

The Botanist and I settled into a routine of seeing each other once or twice a month, until one day I walked into his bedroom to find a young man with a Herculean body waiting on the bed. He was so handsome, he looked surreal. I thought, for a moment, that perhaps the Botanist had put something in my drink.

The Botanist answered the question on

my face with a lurid smile. "I want to watch you fuck him with that black dick of yours."

I shrugged, took off my clothes, and climbed onto the bed. He was a beautiful man, there was no denying it. Tall with a football player's physique, he wore his brown hair long and wild. In the Botanist's blue-lit bedroom full of potted trees and ferns, he looked — well, he looked like Tarzan. The Botanist's ability to create a scene was disturbingly skillful.

And this stranger wanted to be used, so I obliged.

I fucked him hard, then harder, until he started moaning, then growling. Soon, we were both shining with sweat. Just when it was getting hot enough for me to forget that the Botanist was sitting at the foot of the bed, I realized something was off. The guy hadn't cleaned himself out well. Shit was all over the sheets. All over him. All over me. Disgusted, I jumped off the bed and ran to the shower.

With the water running, I started sobbing. The dam in my chest unleashed everything I'd held back for months. When the Botanist climbed into the shower with me, ignoring my tears, or satisfied by them, he grabbed my dick. I was too defeated to stop him. I felt like my body wasn't mine when it was in another man's hands. When he got me hard again and guided my dick inside him, I pushed in from behind. If the Botanist noticed that I was still softly crying as I pressed my body against his, he didn't say a word.

14

September 2007
Bowling Green, Kentucky

Let's call this one Dane.

"Let's play a game," I announced. I was sitting in the passenger seat, locking and unlocking my door out of boredom. Dane raised his eyebrows. He was up to play. So I told him the rules of the Question Game, which were, of course, just my rules.

"We take turns asking each other a question and we have to answer the question, no matter what. I'll go first."

I waited a second. I wondered how far ahead Dane could see into what I was doing, whether he could guess that whenever I decided to play this game it was because I already had a very specific question in mind.

"We're almost to my apartment," he stuttered.

"It won't take long. Okay, first question. What are your favorite kinds of tits?"

Straight guys loved this question. They always laughed the same kind of laugh when they heard it, and usually gave a little sigh of relief as if to say, "Shit, man. I thought you were going to ask some kind of fag question." Sometimes that's what they actually said.

Dane had already launched into a passionate monologue, about why size was overrated, how natural perkiness was what really mattered once the bra came off, and don't even get him started on the rarity of evenly shaped tits, or how nipples are just so unpredictable — I wasn't listening. I was deciding my next move, which questions I would need to ask before we got to his apartment in order to get to the only question I cared about. I figured it would only take two more questions, maybe three.

"Okay, okay, I've got one," Dane said. "What does it feel like . . . you know, fucking a dude?"

I had to give him credit. I hadn't expected this one until we got a little further along. Looking out my window, as if we were talking about great deals on gas prices, I gave my stock answer. "It feels so fucking good."

"Yeah?"

"Oh yeah."

His posture had changed. We were pulling

162

into the parking lot of his apartment complex now. Dane looked up at the lit windows of his two-bedroom. His roommate must have been home; I was losing him. I skipped ahead. "My turn. Have you ever done anything with a guy?"

"I — well, hmm." He fingered the lock button on his side of the car. "I'm gonna need another drink if we're gonna keep playing this game. Let's go upstairs, man."

He slinked out of his car before I had a chance to read his face. I wanted to see it in his eyes — in the eyes of every straight man I'd marked as mine that season — that I was right, right about how slippery gender, sex, and want really are, to prove that I could shame one straight man after another. And by shaming them — in a way — own them. However temporarily, however falsely. Or maybe I just wanted a distraction from how I felt when my body wasn't pinned against another man's body. It didn't even feel like lust, really. It had a tinge of meanness to it, what I was doing. Spite, even. Like I was teaching one man after another a lesson he maybe didn't need to learn.

Dane walked up the steps to his apartment and I followed, tracing my eyes along his shoulders, then down the back of his T-shirt toward the striped boxers peeking every time he took a step. When he unlocked the door to his apartment, the Notorious B.I.G.'s voice throbbed in surround sound.

"Surround sound, my man!" he shouted, dropping his keys on a glass stand. "Let's do some shots."

He was back to himself. All the work I had done in the car seemed to have vanished, and then there was a bottle of Bacardi 151 in one hand and shot glasses in the other. Then one shot and another shot, and two more because we were tired of feeling our legs, and another two because his roommate had joined us.

I swam to the kitchen sink to pour myself a glass of water, but by the time I got there, I couldn't remember why I was alone in the kitchen of a brightly lit apartment that wasn't mine. The bottle of Bacardi, which mere moments ago had been full, sat on the counter empty.

When I found myself back in the living room, Dane and his roommate were on the couch, playing a basketball video game on a huge flat-screen television. The graphics and sound were so impressive, I fell into a lull amid the sounds of cheering fans, sneakers on polished wood floors, referee whistles, and Dane and his roommate heckling each other as they played. I watched them for a moment, both errant frat boys, elbowing each other, mashing thumbs down on their controllers. I closed my eyes and eased back into the folds of Dane's leather couch. Then a silence struck the room, as violent as feedback from a stereo. Biggie was still playing, but the game was on pause.

I blinked and sat up, confused by the interruption. Dane and his roommate sat with their controllers in their hands, eyes wide, shocked by something. They kept looking at each other, then back at me. Just before I opened my mouth to ask what was going on, I played back the last bit of conversation in my head. An "err" sound. Why would a conversation end with an —

"Did one of you say 'nigger'?"

They both sprang back into action, pointing at each other, blaming each other like two little boys trying to escape the blame for a broken vase.

"Why would you even say 'nigger'?"

They both winced each time I said the word so I said it again, not angry, exactly, but not amused either.

"What does 'nigger' have to do with anything that's happening here?"

"A player on my team messed up a play," Dane finally confessed, with the bashfulness of a nine-year-old Klansman.

His roommate got up and walked toward the kitchen without another word. I watched him walk out of the room. All the basketball players on screen, most of them black men, were frozen in place. One player looked like he was about to crash into the floor face-first. The orange ball hovered in midair, refusing to fall.

"Let's go," I said, standing up and remembering, suddenly, that I was wasted.

"Where?"

"Away."

We swam back through the living room and out into the evening. Inside the car, Dane started the engine and off we sped.

"I don't want to go back to campus. Let's just keep driving."

I took him back to the Question Game. He kept driving; we kept talking. With each volley it became a little more difficult to remember why, just moments ago, I had been furious with Dane. "Nigger" dissolved back into an "err" sound, a memory that could be washed out with enough alcohol, enough sex. I can't remember any of the slurred questions we slid back and forth across the purring car — only that it was now foreplay without pretense.

I also can't remember when I started to

166

unzip Dane's jeans. He held up his arms so I could reach in without disturbing his already questionable driving. With his dick in my hand, I chuckled. When he started to ask what I thought was so funny, I swallowed his dick to the hilt, replacing his half-uttered question with a surprised moan.

He pulled over and put the car in Park. We were in a warehouse district on the outskirts of town. Dane reclined his seat. I came up for air and tried to kiss him. Maybe he let me kiss him. That's a blurry memory too. Just before I went back down, I saw a figure on the other side of the road, several yards away. A man, maybe, all shadows. I shrugged and went back down. I felt electric in the way I always did when I had finally won a guy over. Fevered. Dane let out a moan, his head slowly turning from left to right. The windshield was totally fogged. I came up to kiss Dane again and the man was closer now, a couple of yards away from the driver's-side door, if that.

"I don't want you to panic," I started, easing back into my seat. "But there's a guy watching us."

Dane went from silent to panicked in half a second. It would've been hilarious if it weren't so clear he was about to try to speed off. With his jeans tangled about his ankles, his seat halfway reclined and the windshield impossible to see out of, he started screaming about "getting caught" and threw the car into Drive. The instant the car's engine roared back to life was also the instant I noticed an electrical box just ahead of us. A big, metal, unmovable box, perfectly aligned with my side of the car. I didn't have my seat belt on. I saw what was going to happen just a few clicks before it happened. We were already jutting forward, the car's tires peeling as they tried to gain traction on the dew-slick grass.

We crashed into the box head-on, and the force of it sent our untethered bodies flying. Arms waving above my head, mouth open in mid-scream, my body's two-foot journey from passenger seat to dashboard felt like it took hours. My life didn't flash before my eyes so much as a stinging, embarrassed awareness that this could very well be the end. My jeans were unzipped; my dick, limp now, was hanging out of my open fly. I reeked of Bacardi 151 on a Tuesday night. This is how whoever found my body would find me; this is how my last moments would be described to my mother.

My chin slammed into the car's dashboard, then the force of the collision threw me back into my seat, knocking the air out of my lungs. The taste of iron filled my mouth as Dane put the car in reverse and peeled out again. Wrecked, but apparently still alive, we sped back onto the road. I didn't think to look behind us to see if the man was still in the parking lot.

Blood pooled in the space between my gums and lip. I swallowed and it welled up again. The front fender of Dane's car scraped along the asphalt as Dane raced toward campus, cursing the entire way.

"I can't get another DUI, Saeed," he cried. "I fucking can't. Fuck. *Fuck!* My car."

I swallowed my blood and kept quiet. The only thing worse than being a disaster is being a disaster with a witness. I pulled my hoodie over my head and tugged the strings as tight as I could without hurting my already throbbing face any more.

Dane pulled in front of my residence hall and barely let me stumble out before speeding off into the fog. The screech of his broken fender echoed through the trees like the car was begging for forgiveness.

I stood and listened, as blood pooled back up in my mouth. I realized I liked the taste.

15

A joke I used to repeat in those days was: Why be happy when you can be interesting? I knew how to be *interesting*. There was power in being a spectacle, even a miserable spectacle. The punch and the line. *Interesting:* sentences like serrated blades, laughter like machine-gun rounds, a drink in one hand, a borrowed cigarette in the other. If you could draw enough glances, any room could orbit around you.

That New Year's Eve, I wound up at a party that was exactly like every party I had ever been to. An iPod hooked up to a pair of speakers, an awkward costume theme I tried and failed to adhere to, and an apartment clogged with white people. The only difference was that I was getting wasted in Phoenix, Arizona, instead of Bowling Green, Kentucky. In the few days I'd been there,

170

I'd concluded that Arizona was perhaps the whitest place I had ever visited. It was like stepping onto the surface of a very well-lit moon.

The party's theme was "The Future," which is why more than half of the people in attendance were wearing some combination of synthetic fabric, aluminum foil, and sunglasses. I hadn't known there would be a theme and the only other shirt I had packed was a blue calico button-down, so I put my dreadlocks into two pigtails and kept telling everyone I was Dorothy. No one found this in any way strange because, of course, this was The Future and all bets are off in the year 2075.

Over the last few years, at college parties just like this one, I'd been an ice queen; I'd been Plato with a boy dressed as Aristotle in tow; I'd been the hot pink negligee all nuns wear under their robes; I'd been Dorothy from Kansas, fake poppy blossoms woven into my dreadlocks. Maybe a theme like The Future was supposed to get us to wonder, starry-eyed, what the future would be like. But I couldn't find it in myself.

Instead, all I could wonder was whether there'd be a future left for any of us. A black man was running to become president of the United States of America, and I was checking the news every morning, anxious, half expecting to read that he'd been assassinated. Lately, I'd been calling home less. I hadn't even told my mom I was going to be in Phoenix for the holiday. A professor who had known me since I was a freshman confronted me in her office just before the fall semester ended. "What happened to you, Saeed? You used to smile." I stared at the professor blankly, then remembered that this was the part where I was supposed to cry, so I cried. The last time I fucked the Botanist, I'd left bruises, broken skin; I deleted his number and told him to delete mine, again.

This was a future I'd have to figure out on my own, but I didn't want to think about it, at least for one more night. I wanted to dance at a huge, messy party and get blackout drunk. In this particular version of The Future, I was one of three out gay men at the party and the other two were dating each other. But I would find a way. I wanted to spend the night in someone else's body or let someone borrow mine.

For the first few hours of the party, either I didn't notice him or the man who would later try to kill me simply hadn't arrived yet. All night, I was a terrific, bright black mess. I stomped, slinked, sauntered in and out of the kitchen to refill my cup or do shots. I shouted orders about songs that should be added to the party's playlist. Out on the porch, smoking cigarettes, then passing around a blunt, I stared at an orange tree just out of reach until I finally plucked off a fruit. It seemed miraculous, oranges in the dead of winter. Then I realized the unseen side of the fruit was rotted, ants pouring out of the ruin like ink.

Looking back, I can see how someone might see me that night and argue that I had it coming — that I had a man like *him* coming. If that someone was America herself, I can understand how she might rattle off a warning. "That black boy has been too hungry for too long. One of these nights he's gonna bite off more than he can chew."

I will say for myself: America, I did the best I could with what I was given.

The man — let's call him Daniel — looked familiar when I saw him from across the room, as if each part of him had been borrowed from some other boy or man I had wanted. Leaning against that wall, dispassionately sipping a beer, he was the kind of quiet I've noticed in certain men and long hungered for: the silence of men who have it all and thus find it all boring, who don't exert the energy necessary to flirt, persuade, or convince because they know America will come crawling to them on hands and knees. I realize now that what I wanted was not just the bodies of such men, but their power and what they could use that power to do to the rest of us. The brutal exertion of will, destiny made manifest by the unspoken threat their muscled bodies and white skin posed. I hungered for the power of the all-American man, the Marlboro Man and the Marlboro Man's firstborn son, the high-school quarterback, the company's future CEO, Ernest Hemingway, John Wayne, Odysseus, Hercules, Achilles, the shield itself, the stone-cut archetype, the goddamned Everyman, the golden boy, the one.

If I couldn't actually be the one myself, I thought I could survive by devouring him whole. The more "straight," the more "masculine," the more I wanted to see him with his legs spread or up, back arched in an orgasm that didn't just bring him pleasure but a warning: In spite of the man you say you are, in the Future I live in, men like me are coming to conquer you and we will take no prisoners. This is what I thought it meant to be a man fighting for his life. If America was going to hate me for being black and gay, then I might as well make a weapon out of myself.

Midnight came and no one noticed. A few people out on the porch tried to stir up a pathetic countdown, a couple of minutes late, spurred into action by firecrackers going off at other parties in the vast apartment complex. Standing alone outside by that orange tree as the sky lit up then went dark again, I had no one to kiss. Now, I was just a sad college student at a random house party in the middle of a college town. I should've been home with my mother and my dog. She'd be sitting in front of the altar now, candles lit, Kingsley nestled at her feet, praying for a good year and, probably, praying for me. My Solo cup was empty.

Daniel and a girl from the party went into a bedroom together. A group of us crowded around the closed door, eager for entertainment now that midnight had passed and we were apparently out of booze. I can't remember how long we stood there, stage-whispering and laughing with our hands over our mouths, before the door opened again and the girl walked out. She was black too. I wonder now what her night must have been like, a black woman partying on the other side of the otherwise all-white room. When she passed me, I felt a chill that, had I been less drunk, probably would've brought me back to myself. Just like the gay couple I'd assiduously been avoiding all night, I'm not sure I had said a word to her since I got to the house. I was smart enough to understand that my loneliness tended to drive me away from people like her and the gay couple rather than toward them, but I wasn't grown-up enough to understand why.

She made her way through the living room and out to the porch without looking at any of us. Like actors in a camp comedy, we stared in her direction until the porch door closed, then turned our heads back to the bedroom in chorus. Daniel was still in bed, sitting up with his back against the head frame, hands almost politely folded on his lap. All he needed was reading glasses and a novel to complete the look.

I heard the laughter before I realized I was the source of the laughter. I was sitting on the edge of the bed, talking to Daniel like I was a doctor visiting a longtime patient. This was me being *interesting;* there was nothing else left to be. He spoke in the most efficient sentences possible, and even then still radiated that intense silence, his voice soft enough to make you want to lean in a little closer. The Greek chorus left us alone.

My eyes raked his bare chest: the color of his nipples, the goose bumps rising on his skin, the sparse hairs sprouting up in the valley of his pecs, the gradients of his summer tan. This too, for the all-American man, is a kind of offering. *Look at the weapon I've made of myself. You want to cut yourself on me, don't you?*

His lips were pressed into the faintest smirk when I looked up. He knew. Satisfied, he slid out of the bed, wearing only his green and yellow plaid boxers. He put his clothes on with his back turned to me so I couldn't see just how much he knew. I picked up his beer from the nightstand and handed it to him as we walked out together, not a couple but a pair nonetheless. We spent the rest of the party at each other's side, the silence a magnetic force.

I left the party without telling anyone where I was going. Daniel invited me to his apartment and led me into what I assumed was his bedroom. I didn't flinch when he locked the door. When I realized that this was not, in fact, his bedroom, but an empty room with a few boxes in a corner, I shrugged. I wasn't about to turn back.

I started taking off my clothes. Daniel undressed, and the smell of sweat and beer flooded my nostrils. I paused to look him over, but he impatiently pulled my pants off for me. Daniel took me into his mouth and then took over completely. If I hadn't already known the word "straight" was a lie, I knew it then. In my experience, straight men never took the initiative when they had sex with other men. They needed to be seduced or tricked into doing what they had really wanted to do all along; or they needed to *believe* they had been seduced or tricked into being the kind of straight men who suddenly find other men's dicks in their mouths. Daniel, apparently, was different.

He got on top of me and started kissing me, scraping my neck with his teeth. His bites were like sweet little cigarette burns. His urgency was cute, if a bit overwhelming.

He wanted this — not *me,* I knew better — he wanted what we were finally doing. He'd probably wanted this for a very long time. It was difficult to breathe with his body bearing down on me but he, in turn, was what I had wanted all night long: a body, a football player's build, a real man's body.

The straightest thing about him was how

terrible he was at giving head. I didn't mind, though. For me, Daniel was the point, not the sex. I saw him. I watched and waited and now I had him.

Somehow, the blow job got worse. I thought, smiling to myself, *Straight guys really* are *terrible at this. It feels like he's hitting me.* And then, in a flicker of clarity, harsh as a flash bulb, I realized he *was* hitting me.

Daniel went from sucking me to punching me so quickly I could still feel my erection pressed against his stomach. His arms came down from above like lightning bolts. Trapped underneath, all I could do was watch the storm.

In that moment, I shrank into the distance, looking down as two men struggled in a dark room. It wasn't like he was beating me, exactly. He was beating the desire I had brought out in him, shoving it back down to where it usually hid. There, on the floor under him, when I looked up at Daniel, I didn't see a gay basher; I saw a man who thought he was fighting for his life.

Like a driver too drunk to tense up as his car collides with another, I was too drunk to realize I was the one who was supposed to be fighting. Or maybe I knew and still didn't care. I raised my arms to block his punches, tried to hold his fists in mine. I floated in and out of focus, and then I noticed that Daniel was talking. His voice deep, slurred, and low now.

"You're already dead," he said. "You're already dead. You're already dead." His voice sounded strange, like he was underwater. "I'm so evil. I'm so evil. I'm so evil," he said. He repeated each phrase without so much as a pause. He looked up at me again, fearful, distraught, pleading. "I'm so evil." He shook his head left and right, then pulled his fist toward his face as if to wipe away tears. He was crying, I realized. I wanted to hold him. I wanted to pull his body against my own and tell him that I felt broken too, even evil sometimes.

I almost let go so I could wrap my arms around him, but as I moved he bit my thumb, smiling as his teeth sought to draw blood. I yanked back in pain and he laughed a lost, wild laugh. "I'm so evil. I'm so evil. You're already dead." I struggled to grab his fist again before he could land another punch.

We may have been wrestling in that room for minutes or hours. I couldn't tell. He would struggle, then tire, his arms going slack for a moment, then striking out again just when I thought he'd exhausted himself.

I kept ahold of his hands, pushing back every time he tried to batter me. I couldn't let go but I was starting to think about it. Releasing his fists was all I would have to do. I could let my head and body fall back into the room's dark water and he would swim through me, past me, beyond me.

His slurred chants rose and hushed, his arms went slack and stirred. Finally they stayed slack. I risked letting go of his hands and looked at him again. He was snoring between my legs, flat on his stomach, boxer shorts hanging around one of his ankles. As I pulled myself out from under him, I looked down and realized that my dick was still hard and that spurts of cum were drying on my stomach.

Without dressing, I unlocked the room's door and walked into the kitchen. Kneeling beside him again with a glass of water, I tried to prop Daniel up against my knee so he could drink without choking. The water went in one side of his mouth and spilled out the other onto the floor. I eased him back down and stood up.

If standing over the unconscious body of a man who, just moments before, had tried to bash my head in is the closest I will ever come to feeling like a god, I can say now that I understand how a god might look down at a mortal man and love him all the more, precisely because of his vulnerability. There was no part of Daniel left to hide from me. I'd seen how much he wanted another man; I'd seen the storm he'd been struggling his entire life to contain; I'd seen how much he feared and raged against himself; I'd seen so much more of myself in him than I ever could've expected when I first saw him. I didn't know real men hurt the way I'd been hurting.

"What did you do for New Year's Eve?" my mother asked when she called in the morning. My friend had parked his car in front of the departures section at the Phoenix airport. Instead of getting out, I insisted on sitting in the car and talking to my mom. I didn't want her to hear the planes flying overhead.

"I went to a house party," I said. "A lot of people came."

"You sound tired," she said. I thought I heard Kingsley's collar jingling in the background.

"Yeah."

"Well, okay, baby. Drink water. I love you."

"I love you too."

On the flight back to Nashville, I could see a dark blue crescent-moon bruise rising

182

under the skin where Daniel had bit me. I went to the bathroom three times to throw up. Kneeling in the compressed space with my knees on the hard floor reminded my body of being in that dark room. The memory started in my kneecaps then raced through me, lighting up every single ache, scrape, and bruise my body had endured.

16

January 2008
Bowling Green, Kentucky

Who are you the morning after the most beautiful man you have ever kissed tries to kill you? And the morning after that? How about the following week?

Someone from the party uploaded the pictures she had taken on New Year's Eve onto Facebook. Clicking through them one at a time, I leaned toward my computer screen like a forensic scientist. These didn't look like images from what could've been my last night alive. If I hadn't gone to the party myself, I'm not sure I would have even known that these were photos of a New Year's Eve party. Had there even been a theme, or did The Future just mean wearing more black and white than usual? I tried to read my face but its language was inscrutable. I didn't look *interesting*. I didn't look like a man who was screaming behind his smile. I just looked drunk, stoned, and sweaty.

Daniel isn't in any of those pictures. I can't tell you how many times, in the years since, I've gone back through them, hoping and fearing that I will see him, perhaps just out of focus, staring back at me. But he's never there.

I caught myself in the days afterward wishing I had a black eye, a broken bone, or a few more cuts and scrapes, if only to confirm that what I believed had happened in Phoenix had *undeniably* happened. I wanted to look how I felt: somehow both drowned and washed up, a survivor and a whore who got exactly what he deserved.

"Deserved." I started circling that word like dirty water whirling down a drain. As I saw it, I had pursued Daniel for much of that night, hoping that he would invite me back to his place. I had seen him as a sexual object, or rather, I had built a metaphor around his body. And then, once we were alone in that room, he broke out of it, and almost broke me. Did I deserve what had happened to me? Had I been asking for it? Had I pushed too far? Or was this simply the risk I accepted, and would have to continue to accept, any time I went back to a guy's place?

As the days went on, I did everything I could to avoid taking the time to answer these questions. Instead, I tried to write past them. I thought productivity was what survival looked like. At the time I had been applying to MFA programs; I had been trying to finish poems; I had been imagining myself as a writer and mostly failing.

The next week, sitting in the Writing Center, waiting for a student I was supposed to tutor, I opened a blank Word document on my computer and started writing what I quickly decided was a "nonfiction short story" — about a black gay writer who goes to a New Year's Eve party in Phoenix, meets a straight guy, and goes home with him. I wrote so quickly I didn't even notice that the student hadn't bothered to show up for his appointment. I just kept writing.

When I had to go to class, I started writing in my notebook instead. I wrote in the library stacks between classes or until the librarian announced closing time on the crackling intercom. I wrote until the crescent-moon bruise Daniel's teeth had left on my thumb started to throb; I wrote until the throbbing went away.

The story was a retelling of that night's events, mostly accurate until just before the end. The writer and the straight man wrestle in that dark room until the writer's head is bashed against the floor one final time, one time too many. As he dies, the writer narrates the rest of the story while he looks down at his body, sprawled in a pool of blood. The straight man unlocks the door and leaves. He doesn't even bother to run.

I believed that I could control any story I told. If something happened, I could write about it, own it, resolve it. Simple. You could afford to be interesting if you could pin everything to the page afterward. Perhaps just to prove how tough I was, I had turned a nightmare of a near miss into a fatal one in my retelling. *See? I'm not scared or weak. I'm not afraid to push through what happened and on into what could have happened.*

I needed to turn in a piece for a creative writing workshop so I submitted the story. It had been less than two weeks since the attack. I didn't have nightmares about that dark room. I didn't cry. Instead, I wrote and insisted that each new draft multiplied the miles and days between me and that room in Phoenix. But when it was time to discuss my story in the workshop, my classmates were mostly baffled. The assignment had been to write a nonfiction essay so how could the narrator — presumably me — die at the end? One of the workshop's rules was that you couldn't talk while your work was being discussed. It was just as well. While my classmates tried to make sense of the perspective or the tense, I listened without hearing them. Daniel had been wrong when he told me I was dead. I felt my classmates were wrong too. They couldn't see what I had survived.

But then maybe I was wrong too. On one level, I knew I needed to write it out. On another, every time I saw a man on campus now who reminded me of Daniel, and damn near every man did, my hands would clench into fists. *If a man ever puts his hands on me like that again,* I'd think, *I will kill him. I won't be able to stop myself.* Even as I'd leashed Daniel to the page, he wouldn't stay there.

A year later, I was in the MFA program at Rutgers–Newark. I had gotten in. I had kept writing. I had escaped and survived. I had proven — to myself, to others — that I could do it. Yet still, so much inside me kept roiling, half contained, like a dam waiting to burst.

I was in a coffee shop one afternoon, at my favorite corner table, with a pile of books in front of me. I had come here, as I often did, to read, take notes, and revise poems before walking to campus. The storm in my chest started the way all my storms do: I exhaled, then inhaled, but there was a little less air in my lungs than had been there before. I exhaled, inhaled again, even less air this time. Looking up from my book, I scanned the shop, hoping no one had noticed the panic attack quickly taking hold. *Exhale, inhale.* My poetry workshop was in a couple of hours. *Exhale, inhale.*

I had just highlighted a sentence in the Reginald Shepherd essay I was reading, about why he writes — or why he *had* written. "My aim is to rescue some portion of the drowned and drowning, including always myself."

I couldn't quite place it, but something about that sentence sent me spinning. Shepherd had died a few months before, just after turning forty-five. One thought, *exhale,* led to another, *inhale,* and another, *exhale,* and another. My heart was a bruised fist, knocking about my rib cage. I leaned forward, looking at the books and my notes again.

My notebook was a graveyard of poets: Melvin Dixon: dead, 1992. Essex Hemphill: dead, 1995. Joseph Beam: dead, 1988. Assotto Saint: dead, 1994. Reginald Shepherd: dead, 2008. The names ran together as I blinked back tears. The names became my name. It's just too easy for a gay black man to drown amid the names of dead black gay men. Since I had started my graduate studies, it seemed that just as soon as I looked up the name of a gay black poet whose work I aspired to one day see my own work read alongside, I'd learn that the poet had died of AIDS, or poverty, or some other tragedy that left him abandoned on the margins of literature's memory.

I stood unsteadily and walked to the restroom, biting my lip, staring at my feet as I moved, to keep from falling apart altogether in front of the baristas, the college students, and the professors cheerily chatting around me. It was like being a teenager again in the Lewisville Public Library, sitting cross-legged on the floor with my hands trembling as I paged through all the books I could find about being gay. Book after book about gay men dying of AIDS. After having put so many years and miles between the scared little boy and the young man I had fought so hard to become, here I was again: alone in the crowd, the black kid trembling in the middle of a graveyard only he could perceive. "The drowned and the drowning, including always myself."

Alone in the restroom, I leaned toward my reflection in the mirror above the sink and sneered. *Just stop,* I thought. *Those names are not your name.* But it was too late now. Memory pulled me under and down into that dark room in Phoenix. I could feel my body pinned under Daniel's weight. My head ached as if it had just been banged against the wood floor.

I slammed my eyes shut to make him and myself disappear. How had he found me here? It had been so long since I had even thought about that night. I didn't see Daniel hiding in other men's shadows anymore. I had walked out of that room and written about it. I wrote about him, then past him — one poem, one story, one essay at a time. Pen as weapon, page as shield. But what was the point of beating him back, only to look up all this time later and feel that history itself was shouting: "You're already dead, you're already dead, you're already dead"?

I stood in front of the mirror, sobbing, unable to stop myself.

Boys like us never really got away, it seemed. We just bought ourselves time. A few more gasps of air, a few more poems, a few more years. History hurt more than any weapon inflicted on us. It hit back harder than any weapon we could wield, any weapon we could turn ourselves into.

I sunk down, I looked away, I felt that loneliness and let it settle in, heavy and final. I don't know how long I sat on the floor in that restroom, staring and seeing nothing. Eventually, I stood up again and washed my face, still avoiding my reflection. It seemed as if my life were waiting for me outside that room, like a polite guest I'd left behind at the table. It was rude to keep him waiting. It helped to think of my life as someone separate from me, a person who didn't deserve to be abandoned.

Sitting back down in front of the pile of books, I returned to Reginald Shepherd's words: he was gone but they were still here. I thought about all the poets who had kept me going, one more minute, one more step. *Of the drowned and the drowning.* I felt the cord pull taut between us. I took a breath. I started a draft of a new poem.

■ ■ ■ ■

PART FOUR

■ ■ ■ ■

When we lived in Dallas on Northwest Highway, we had gone to the Tom Thumb on a cold, wintery Friday night for groceries. I chanted that the check I wrote would be approved. I remember putting the groceries in the kitchen and you were in the den watching TV. I just started crying. I wanted to give up. I was so tired and depressed about raising a child alone and always worried about paying the bills and putting food on the table. I knew if I made a phone call to my mom, she would take over raising you in a heartbeat. The thought was so loud in my heart and mind to just "give up" and move into a smaller place alone.

I went to the altar and chanted through silent tears because I did not want to upset you. I can't imagine how both our lives would have been if I did not have that hope in my heart to keep going and do whatever possible to keep us together. I know for sure I have absolutely no regrets for you in my life.

Love forever,
Mama
February 5, 2007

17

April 2011
Jersey City, New Jersey
4:45 a.m., Monday. My coffee maker had its own alarm clock, clicking itself awake fifteen minutes before me, and three hours before first period. Moving, but still not awake exactly, I'd walk across my studio apartment, the smell of coffee wafting around me, and pour myself the first of two cups.

As I sipped that first cup of coffee, I'd light the two candles in front of my altar and start chanting. Sitting cross-legged on the rug next to my bed, I'd chant nammyoho-renge-kyo for forty-five minutes. I'd chant for my twelfth-grade students to get into college. I'd chant to be able to write another poem. I'd chant for it to be good. I'd chant for my mother. My mind would drift like a boy wading into a river, the current gently pulling at his waist. The sun was

195

not up yet. My street was silent. I'd check my watch and, after forty-five minutes, blow out the candles.

I would pour myself another cup of coffee, then sit down at my desk to write. I wrote poems on the back of old lesson plans; this made it easier to ball up the failed ideas and throw them away. I'd pick up another sheet and write a line. *The blue dress is a river.* I'd stop, draw a dash, and try again. *The blue dress is a silk train is a river.*

I dressed. I put a book in my bag to read during my lunch break. I locked my front door. I went to the high school in Newark where I worked. My ninth-grade students were reading *The Catcher in the Rye.* They loved Holden. I thought, *Well, of course, they* love *Holden. They're ninth graders.*

As usual, after I dismissed them for lunch, I'd pull out the lunch I packed for myself and a poetry collection to read while I sat at my desk. I did this every day during the week; I worked on my poems for forty-five minutes every morning for fear that if I didn't make a constant effort, I'd look up one day and five or six years would have passed without me having published a single poem, much less an actual book. Same with the lunchtime reading. Even though I was too tired to understand everything I was taking in, I forced myself to run my eyes over the entirety of two poems before I allowed myself to put the book down. This was the routine. I needed to use all the time I had. I needed to keep kicking to stay afloat.

Often, with the book facedown in front of me, I'd text Mom about my day, maybe send her a picture of the pile of homework assignments on the corner of my desk waiting to be graded. I was proud of my exhaustion, as if the darkness circling my eyes was proof of my adulthood. Proof that I could hold my own, no longer just a son or grandson but an I.

This day in April, Mom texted me first: "Could you call me later?"

I felt a spark of panic. I put my phone back down and picked up the book, gripping it a little tighter. Over the last year, Mom had needed help with money, and I knew that asking me couldn't have been easy. Her "Could you call me later?" texts gave me the same ache I felt when people used to tell me that I was "the man of the house," spawning a swarm of mosquito-like questions in my head. *Was everything okay? What did she need to talk about on the phone? Was it her health or money? Do I even have any money saved up right now?*

After work, I went home, poured myself a glass of wine, and climbed into bed with my laptop, intending to watch a movie. "Are you home from work yet? Call me." I'd been pretending to ignore the ache in my chest but I couldn't anymore. I was ashamed that I hadn't already called her back. Downing the last of the wine in my glass, I dialed her number.

"I want you to meet me in Memphis for your grandmother's birthday," she said as soon as she answered, as if we were already several minutes into the conversation. I had expected her to sound pained, but there was a song in her voice, wrapped around steel.

"Hi, Mom."

"Well?"

"Isn't her birthday really soon?"

"You can fly in this Saturday. We'll take her to lunch and you can fly back that night or the next morning."

She had already looked up flights we could take for free using her employee benefits at Delta. She had already picked out a restaurant too. It was a little funny to see my mother as the devoted daughter, but also frustrating. I'd been making up excuses to avoid going to Memphis for so long that it actually took a bit of effort to remember why I stayed away. But I still hadn't forgiven my grandmother. Even as I felt the pull of Mom's eagerness, I tried to resist the current.

"My lesson plans are due on Sunday afternoon," I said. "You know that." I yawned, because I was tired and because I wanted her to hear that I was tired.

"Saeed, I'm not asking," she chimed. "I'm telling."

It was a line she had been using on me since I was a little boy. It was partly a joke, but really not. It was an announcement that the discussion was over and decided. In fact, it had been over and decided well before I answered the phone. She knew it, and now I knew it too. I might as well have already been on the airplane.

"Okay," I said, "but you owe me."

"Sedrick Saeed Jones, quit playing. I *made* you." She laughed then hung up. I wanted to laugh too, but I felt swept along, swept past. It annoyed me, how easily she was able to pry me away from myself. When I put down the phone, though, my frustration curdled into shame. How could I begrudge the woman who raised me on her own? How dare I, when she had found it in herself to keep loving her own mother through decades of ups and downs?

My mom liked to say "we don't eat coconut cake in this family," as if we were the kind of family who created traditions and stuck to them. We weren't. No family reunions; no silly nicknames with winding back-stories; no annual family vacations. We did, at least, have a family story about coconut cake. As my grandmother tells it, in 1968, she had just started to slide her knife into the coconut cake the family had made for her birthday when a woman in the living room started wailing. The radio in that room had just cut to breaking news. The announcer said that Martin Luther King Jr. had been shot and killed downtown. Everyone stood stunned until that woman — a neighbor from down the street — started screaming. My grandmother set down her plate, the piece of cake untouched. She knew that woman was just going to keep on wailing until someone went in there and calmed her down.

It had been years since I'd heard the story, but I thought about it often. The sweetness we deny ourselves because the world is wailing. Now, in the car on our way to brunch, my grandmother retold it once again. I found myself drawn in, giving her all my attention for the first time since I was a little boy. "That neighbor was always so dramatic," my grandmother said, eyeing the curb while Mom parked the car. "Always fussing and carrying on."

After we parked, Mom got out, walked over to the passenger side, and helped Grandma get out of the car. Wrapping their arms around each other, mother and daughter rose, then slowly walked into the café. Mom whispered something. I followed behind with my aunt Celia, scrolling through pictures of my studio apartment in Jersey City for her.

"See?" Mom said, allowing her mother to lean into her weight. "It's easier to walk like this, isn't it? This is how it would be with a cane." I couldn't hear if my grandmother answered but it sounded like another installment in a conversation the two of them had been having for months. Mom was flying to Memphis from Atlanta most weekends now to visit her mother. She was thinking about moving there full-time. Whenever the topic came up, I changed the subject or got quiet until she changed it. For most of the afternoon, my grandmother and I had barely spoken beyond the initial hellos and hugs. We talked through my mother and my aunt, filtering our conversation between them, politely pretending not to notice how consistently the two of us avoided making eye contact.

It was a bright spring afternoon. Tulips lined the outdoor café, drooping their heads. My mother ordered mimosas for everyone, even though my grandmother rarely if ever drank.

Was soul music playing at the café that day? I can't remember. I only remember the insistence of my mother's smile and laughter, and how I felt the urge to resist it — to prove a point and send a dark cloud over the day. But then, I couldn't do it.

Maybe she was the music I'm trying to recall now. My mother's mood caught us like a Bill Withers chorus. My grandmother burped, looking at her mimosa as if betrayed. Then she giggled, decades falling from her face for a moment. Mom and my aunt started laughing too. I smirked, at first just trying to be a good sport. But then the laughter settled into an irresistible rhythm. I bumped my shoulder into Aunt Celia, our heads leaning against each other's for a moment. How many mimosas had we had? We all laughed louder.

Even now, I can hear it. I can hear the music ringing out. I can see my mother at the head of the table: the only one who could bring us all together, the only one who could tune us into any semblance of harmony. The sweetness was ours that day and, for once, no one at the table denied it.

18

May 7, 2011
Jersey City, New Jersey

The night before Mother's Day, I was in bed watching a TV show on my laptop, willfully avoiding the lesson plans I needed to finish. On my screen, a businessman stood in the middle of a barren field, begging the stranger standing behind him with a pistol not to pull the trigger. The shot rang out. The man fell to his knees.

My phone started to ring.

My uncle Albert was calling from Memphis. Seeing his name on the phone's screen brought a burst of irritation. *What now?* I thought. *I don't have time for this.* My uncle and I usually spoke once or twice a year, if that, mostly birthdays and holidays. He probably wanted to remind me about Mother's Day and to call all the women in my family like a good son, a good nephew, a good grandson. Mom was in Memphis, celebrating with my grandmother. I watched my uncle's name flash on the phone's screen, arguing with him in my head. I didn't need a reminder to call my own mother on Mother's Day. I would call everyone in the morning when I woke up.

His name flickered again and then went dim. I turned the phone facedown. It was none of his business that I hadn't planned far enough ahead to mail Mom a gift or card this year. It was my first year working full-time, trying to make good on undergrad and grad school. I was busy; she understood.

I hit Play on my laptop. The businessman was still on his knees, looking up at the bright blue sky as if noticing a halo above his head, then he fell face first into the mud. My phone rang again; Uncle Albert again.

I realized people don't call that late at night to just nag. I answered.

"Saeed," my uncle said, his voice calm but firm, as if he'd heard the silent argument we'd just had. "Your mother is in the emergency room. After dinner tonight, she had trouble breathing and went to the hospital. I'll call you back as soon as I know more."

I said, "Okay," then waited for more words to come. But they didn't. My uncle hesitated for a moment, perhaps waiting for me to say something else, to overwhelm him with frantic questions. He took a breath then hung up.

The businessman was still facedown in the mud. His killer was off screen. It felt like someone was standing in the corner of my apartment now, a silent judge taking note of my every move and expression. I slid out of bed, careful not to knock over the glass of cheap red wine on the floor, and walked to my altar. *That corner,* I decided. The person I couldn't see must be standing in *that corner.* Turning back to face the altar, I lit the candles and started chanting, surprised to hear words actually leaving my mouth.

When she was worried, my mother could chant for hours without stopping. For weeks at a time, she would wake up early and chant for two, even three hours before getting dressed for work. And when she got home at the end of the day, she would sit right back in front of her altar and start chanting all over again. Eviction notices on the kitchen counter, a car that had broken down the day before, prescriptions for heart medication that needed to be refilled despite an overdrawn checking account, a gay son living on his own hundreds of miles away.

She chanted until the Sanskrit words became abstract sounds, until the sound itself became unnoticeable. Like crickets chirping outside your window on a spring evening, the sound of my mother's prayers just became the night itself.

I looked at my watch. Less than five minutes had passed. I couldn't chant for hours; I wasn't like my mother. My mind would start to drift, slipping into unexpected memories and anxieties, blurring the past, present, and unreal until I needed to stop and check the time. When I was a teenager, kneeling or sitting cross-legged in front of the altar for even thirty minutes would give me cramps. Mom would swat my thigh when I prayed with her, my legs sprawled out on the carpet like I was a life-size rag doll. She could always tell when I was starting to drift off.

Blowing out the candles, closing the altar's wooden doors, I thought about the night she drove herself to the ER in Lewisville, just hours before driving that U-Haul truck for nearly twelve hours nonstop to Atlanta. My family didn't understand the kind of woman my mother had become. She wasn't like them, or me. She was stronger.

I got back in bed, hit Rewind, and watched the businessman get shot all over again.

Nothing had changed. It comforted me to see him fall to the ground exactly like he'd fallen the first time. He was locked in a story and it went on according to plan. My mother and I were in a story too, I remember thinking. This night would, in the end, just be one Sanskrit word uttered in a very long prayer. I slept well that night, but I didn't dream.

The next morning, my uncle called before my alarm clock went off. I knocked over the empty wineglass when my feet hit the floor and, I swear, by the time I reached down to pick it up I was on an airplane flying toward Memphis.

"Saeed, your mother is in a coma," he had said. "You need to find a way to get here." She had gone into cardiac arrest just after the ambulance arrived at the hospital. More than twenty minutes passed before doctors were able to get her heart back into a regular pattern. Time held her brain hostage for each of those minutes. Her body went into a coma in reaction to the trauma.

I can't remember my uncle speaking these words, though surely he must have been the first person to explain what had happened. I didn't know any of this and then it was all I knew. When the flight attendant asked me to turn off my phone, I was tempted to ask her to speak louder, to shout over the other sentence — couldn't she hear it? — "Saeed, your mother is in a coma."

A man in his thirties sat next to me on the flight. When he slid past me, I smelled sandalwood, and I hated myself for noticing. *How can you be thinking that at a time like this?* a voice shouted in my head. Even the most banal ideas and gestures seemed to turn against me, transformed by the idea that there was a certain way to "be" in a crisis. It was like I was learning how to be a man again — and already failing. The good son, the good nephew, the good grandson. If only someone would give me the script so I could perform my role accordingly. Without it, I found myself stunned into silence, fearful that my next word, thought, or action would be the last coin dropped onto the scale, tipping me toward judgment. The punishment, I assumed, would be my mother's worsening condition.

The passenger leaned toward me at one point, holding out his phone, swiping through pictures from a recent ski trip. I ordered a Bloody Mary, and then I ordered another Bloody Mary. Did he make a joke about also needing a stiff drink on Mother's Day? What kind of man . . . *Mother's Day.* I hadn't thought about it until just then. He asked what I had planned for my trip in Memphis and I said that my mother was sick and I was going to check on her. He nodded, eyes lowered, then changed the subject: Did I have a boyfriend, *Saeed, your mother is in a coma,* where in town would I be staying, *Saeed, your mother is in a coma.*

Walking off the plane and down the Jetway toward the gate, I thought about how Mom and I had been flying in and out of this airport since my very first flight. Back when families could still meet arriving passengers at the gate, my grandmother would meet us there amid the crowd. "I could hear you just laughing and talking the whole way," she would say, teasing us. "I just said, 'Yep, Carol and Saeed.' My baby and her baby, as loud as can be." And we'd hug and laugh again. Her accent always pooled a little extra honey into the vowels of our names.

Alone this time, I walked through the memory of that laughter. My uncle and his wife picked me up outside baggage claim. Loading my suitcase into the back of their SUV, I realized that I'd only brought a backpack and a small weekend suitcase. I couldn't even remember what I'd packed that morning. Sliding into the backseat, I smiled, even joked, making small talk. My aunt told me she liked my sunglasses. When my uncle said that we should probably go directly to the hospital, I inhaled and nodded.

The hallways in the hospital hummed with silence, occasionally shot through with the sound of violent coughing from a patient in one of the dark rooms we passed. When we reached the ICU, my legs started to stiffen and shudder. A nurse at the station nodded at my uncle and smiled at me. The look of someone who knows the next sentence of your story before you do. My aunt decided to wait in the hallway. And then my uncle put his hand on my shoulder, guiding me toward one of the rooms. The tenderness of his touch set off a serpentine chill through my body. If he was being this gentle, it was because he knew I needed to be prepared for what I was about to see.

We stepped into the hushed room together, but as I approached the bed, I felt that I was on my own. I cannot tell you who I thought I saw sleeping there, surrounded by machines, wires and tubes snaking in and out of her body. *Poor woman, lonely stranger. Where is her family? Is there someone we can call?*

I looked at my uncle and he nodded, as if understanding the question in my eyes. We *were* the ones who had been called. We stood close enough for my hands to rest on the bed's rails. I hesitated to touch her. My uncle started speaking to her as I stared. With two fingers, he smoothed a few strands of hair away from her face.

And, like a grim miracle, there she was. My mother's face. My mother's hair. Under her eyes, dark circles: a gift from my grandmother to my mother to me.

I think I tried to talk to my mother then. You know the voice, the way family members speak from the hospital bedside of loved ones. That tone. I tried it, even as I hated it. The pity and desperation, a sickly sweetness clinging to my words, slowing them down, putting pauses in my sentences where I did not mean to be silent. I spoke about my flight, about my uncle picking me up at the airport, about my twelfth graders reading Toni Morrison this unit. I even talked about the weather. Nothing.

"I'm here, Mama. I'm right here," I said, at a loss.

I thought back to the night I visited her in the ER in Lewisville, when she had congestive heart failure. "I can't go back to sleep," she had whispered to the nurse as I stood nearby. "I'm afraid that if I go to sleep I won't wake back up."

As this memory washed over me, I looked up and saw my mother's eyelids start to flutter. I thought she was waking up, as if all she had needed was for her son to stand at her bedside and say "Mama." I thought that maybe we would be okay. Maybe she would need to stay in Memphis for a few weeks to recover, even months. Maybe I could fly back on the weekends to check on her. I'm sure my boss would understand. It would be exhausting, all the back and forth, but we'd figure it out. Maybe the two of us were, in fact, as special as I hadn't before dared to believe.

The machines surrounding us lit up, beeping and flashing. Doctors and nurses rushed into the room as my mother's head started shaking, her whole body writhing as spit foamed at her mouth.

I hadn't even known it was possible for someone in a coma to have a seizure. I stood stunned. I froze, in everyone's way, until my uncle all but picked me up and carried me out of the room. Back in the hallway, I tried to catch my breath as I looked back over my shoulder. My mouth hung open in shock. I tried to walk away but I had no legs, there was no floor. I started to collapse just as my uncle rushed to catch me.

He guided me to a chair and I sat, waiting for the rest of my body to find me. A doctor walked over and explained what had just happened, but I couldn't really hear him. A few minutes later, my uncle and I went back to check on her. The doctors and nurses were gone. She was just a sleeping woman again.

We spoke to her, and I started chanting softly. Or maybe I was just thinking about chanting. I can't remember. Just a few moments later, my mother had another seizure. Doctors and nurses rushed back into the room and this time I ran out. When my uncle found me, I'm not sure who or what he saw, but he guided me down that hallway, past room after room.

Back in his SUV, a city blurred on the other side of the window. I knew my uncle and aunt were talking, but I couldn't make out the words except when she said, "He's just going to need some time, Albert." Sitting in the backseat, I could feel it begin: the outlines of my silhouette beginning to crumble and come apart, the color of my skin and then the flesh itself pooling out like ink dropped into clear water, all swirls and eddies. I was turning into fog. And in me, what had already been difficult —

distinguishing between memory and present moment, between thought and action — became practically impossible. I could've been anywhere; I could've been anything.

I sat at the table in my grandmother's kitchen. When I was a little boy, sometimes I would sit at this perfect dark wooden circle with her and my grandfather for dinner. There used to be a lamp hanging directly over the table and it would start to swing a bit whenever Memphis experienced tremors from the nearby fault line in Arkansas. The lamp would swing back and forth, pushing and pulling our shadows as we ate our food without much conversation. No one bothered to explain why every once in a while, for just a few seconds, the earth would tremble and that lamp would sway. I would look at my grandparents, unable to decipher their silence, and go back to my other pressing concern: if I didn't eat all my food, I would have to sit alone at that table until told otherwise. And so, the three of us would just keep eating. The lamp always exhausted itself.

I had sat at this same table to write a poem the last Christmas my mother and I had visited Memphis together. I would write a line, stop, and write the line over again, changing a word or moving a comma. I loved poetry then, not so much because of language and images but because I enjoyed the control. It was snowing outside the kitchen window. My mother and grandmother were sitting in the living room, and I could catch occasional snippets of their conversation.

"Are you still crying about that dog?" my grandmother asked at one point. I thought I could detect a teasing laugh in her throat, her Memphis accent turning "dog" into "dawg."

The summer before, Kingsley had died, and Mom had taken it especially hard. I hadn't heard my mother crying, but I got up and stood in the kitchen's doorway. Sitting on the couch, Mom wept quietly, her head bent forward as she looked at her hands.

"I miss him," she said softly, in a sudden childlike voice.

Grandma was staring out the window. She was in her favorite chair, her right leg bouncing just a bit, the way it always did when she was thinking but not going to say what she was thinking.

After my grandfather died, sometimes I'd see her sitting on the couch, bouncing her leg for a few minutes before she'd get up and turn on some music — Bill Withers's "Use Me" and Al Green's "Tired of Being Alone" are the songs I remember her playing the most. The opening chords would start and she'd slowly back away from the cassette player, swaying as she gained momentum, and then she was off. She'd dance from room to room, singing along and swaying, the saddest smiling woman I had ever seen.

"Grandma, it wasn't that long ago," I said, standing at the edge of the kitchen. She had been letting the silence grow. "We both still miss him," I said.

Mom had called me right after Kingsley had died, late at night, crying. "I'm holding him right now," she said on the phone. "I picked Kingsley up, brought him into bed with me, and just held him until he stopped breathing."

She'd felt so far away. Maybe, I wondered, if we hadn't been far away from each other that night, I would be as sad as she was about Kingsley dying.

Watching my grandmother continue to bounce her leg and my mother wiping her face, I didn't know what more to say. I decided to step away that day. I didn't know how to explain these two women to each other. They were their own business. I retreated back to the kitchen table and the poem and the snow falling outside the window.

I can't remember if the three of us ever sat at that table together. I didn't have my mother's talent for bringing the family together, soothing us into enjoying one another's company despite ourselves.

Now, after visiting my mother in the hospital, I sat at the table in my grandmother's kitchen because no other part of her house was safe. When we first got to her house, I found her sitting in her favorite chair.

"Hey, baby."

"Hey, Grandma."

I bent down to hug her, kissed her on the cheek. We didn't say much; there wasn't much I felt I *could* say. I didn't want to tell her that her daughter was having seizures while in a coma. My grandmother used to be a nurse; she would know if I were lying about how Mom was doing. I wasn't ready to admit out loud how useless I felt standing beside the sleeping woman.

Instead, Grandma latched on to my uncle, barraging him with questions about where people were and what was happening and what we were going to eat and why hadn't so-and-so returned her call and where was the charger for her cell phone. Being in the same room with her felt like trying to push two magnets together from the wrong ends. A mother terribly worried about her daughter, a son terribly worried about his mother, in wholly incompatible ways.

Retreating to the edge of the living room, I noticed then that she still had mirrors all over the walls. They broke up our bodies and handed them back to us piecemeal.

I decided that I should take a nap and leave the others to themselves.

The moment I opened the guest bedroom's door, I realized my mistake. My mother's open suitcase was at the foot of the bed. Of course. She always stayed here when she came to visit.

I froze mid-step, then I closed the door behind me. On the nightstand, a clear plastic bag held the shredded remnants of the dress doctors must have had to cut my mother out of, some of the bracelets she always wore, and her wallet. I sat the bag down and climbed onto the bed, blinking back tears. One at a time, I grabbed the pillows, pressing my face into them until I found the smell of her hair. I found my mother there, briefly, her perfume mixed with the burn of a curling iron. I held my face against that pillow and screamed.

Before I opened the door and walked out again, I paused to wipe my face. When I put my hand on the doorknob, I thought about her hand touching this very same knob only the day before and I turned to fog again, a wispy almost-man drifting through my grandmother's house, past mirrors that could no longer see me, until I made it back into the kitchen. I sat at the table, staring at nothing until my uncle walked in.

"I can't sleep here," I said, quietly so my grandmother wouldn't hear me. He nodded.

The next morning, I woke up in a twin bed in a room filled with trophies, basketballs, and track cleats. For a moment, I felt like I'd left one dream only to wake up in another. Then I remembered. I stared at the ceiling as the rest of the previous day's memories seeped back into me like an IV drip. This happened every morning for the next few days. Sunlight or my uncle's voice from the doorway would wake me up, I'd smile, bemused to be sleeping in a bed with sports-themed sheets, and then: "Oh, right."

Downstairs, my uncle would tell me to eat and I would eat. He would tell me it was time for us to go to the hospital and we'd go. Sometimes we'd stop by my grandmother's house to pick her or another relative up. Sometimes we'd just go straight there. My mother didn't have any more seizures. It got easier to talk to her. It also got easier for me to comfortably sit in the corner of her room, chanting nam-myoho-renge-kyo with a clear voice. I hoped, as the sons of sleeping women always do, that she heard my voice. Sometimes I'd realize my chanting was falling into the same rhythm as the beeping machines monitoring her and I would stop. I didn't like the idea of my prayers being encased in a rhythm that I couldn't control. Eventually, a nurse would stop by the room to check on her. Occasionally, we'd see the doctor himself, but his visits rarely brought new news or comfort. Nothing had changed. Uncle would then say it was time to go or time to eat or time to make phone calls and I'd do it and I'd do it and I'd do it.

Outside of the routine of my uncle's gentle orders, I couldn't trust myself to stay myself so I tried my best to stay in step. We slipped into a forced waltz, unsure what would happen if either of us ever stopped. People started to arrive. My mom's sister from California, my mom's best friend from Ohio. Sometimes people came because I had called them myself but by the time they showed up, a few hours or a day later, I'd have no memory of having done so. We'd drive from house to house. We'd make more calls. I would walk my cousin's dog so I'd have an excuse to avoid sitting in the living room with my family. I'd sit at this kitchen table or that kitchen table until my uncle would find me staring off into space and tell me I needed to go to sleep. There was nothing to do but wait. The food, the calls, the houses, the tables, the nurses, the coma, the dog, the dreams. Then the doctor said we were running out of options. He pulled charts and brain scans out of a folder. As he spoke, I latched on to what little I could. The trauma of her brain going so long without oxygen had been devastating. The doctor was hoping to see some flicker of activity, proof that the brain was starting to recover.

My uncle walked over to the bed, took my mother's hand, and leaned toward her ear to whisper. "Carol Jean," he said, softly but firmly, a brother encouraging his baby sister, "I know you can hear me. There is a light somewhere in you and I need you to reach out and hold on to it. I know it's there and I know you can find it. I just need you to reach out and hold on to it, okay?"

More people arrived. Extended family

members I hadn't seen in years, longtime friends and coworkers of my mother, people who had first taught her about Buddhism when she was in her twenties. As more friends and family members arrived, the comfort of their presence was cut through by the fact that their arrival was proof that the situation was worsening.

Beyond the initial greeting — gentle smile, hug, and "It's so good to see you" — I wasn't much use. The hospital visits — usually twice a day — seemed to bend time. Our hours revolved around the woman in that bed. Every bite of food, every song fizzling on my grandmother's old radio. Every conversation, however silly or pleasant, was being had now because of something my mother's heart had set in motion. My family visited her in different combinations. Sometimes my grandmother would sit in the chair by the window, bouncing her leg. Sometimes I would chant alone by the bed; other times friends of my mother would join me. During one visit, several nurses stepped into the room to say hello. I thought one of them looked new. Maybe she had switched shifts with one of the regulars. She was a short black woman with brochures in her hand.

"Is it okay if we speak for a moment?" she

said to the room. Everyone made eye contact with one another and then shuffled into the hallway. The Buddhist friends who had first taught my mother how to chant stayed behind in the room and kept chanting quietly.

The nurse I didn't recognize guided us into a little room I hadn't seen before. It had fake stained-glass windows even though the room actually had no windows. I know the doctor was the one to say it, but I have no memory of hearing the words "brain dead" for the first time. As my memory tells it, when I walked into that tiny room, I had a mother and when I walked out, I didn't.

19

May 2011
Memphis, Tennessee

As soon as I was old enough to learn what cigarette smoking did to the body, I started wondering how my mother would end. Sometimes I would try to picture a dark, tobacco-scented flower blossoming in one of her lungs, then another and another, just like the cancer that had killed my grandfather. Maybe the flowers would die off one winter, only to return the following spring. It would be awful, I was sure, but it would be slow. We would have time to say goodbye. We'd watch the season change together.

The sun had gone down by the time we made it back to my uncle's home. One by one, we stepped out of the SUV, red-eyed, exhausted into silence. We held hands a moment longer than usual, patting one another's shoulders or hugging again, before slowly separating. I said that I was going to take the dog for a walk, then left the dog inside and walked out into the dark alone. I realized now that I'd taken to walking the dog several times a day because that's exactly what Mom would've done if she had been here.

The air was noisy with crickets chirping and leaves rustling in the breeze. With my eyes closed, all the trees shifting in the night sounded like faraway ocean waves. I walked slowly down the long, gravel driveway between the house and the road. About halfway, I fell to my knees. I ran my hands through the dirt, pushing the stones, then pulling them back in handfuls as my tears stained them. It didn't matter how I acted anymore.

A friend told me once that after her father died, she cried so intensely, a blood vessel in one of her eyes burst. It had seemed like an impossible marvel when she told me at the time, but now I knew. Tears don't always just fall; sometimes they rip through you, like storm-painted gusts instead of mere raindrops.

There were so many stories about my mother I'd never heard, or rather: my mother had so many stories I'd never thought to ask her to share. Her sister told us, one of those afternoons, that when Mom was a teenager, she plastered an entire side of their bedroom with Jackson 5 posters. She wrote each of them fan letters and then wrote a novel about a black girl who happens to bump into the group on the street in Beverly Hills and is whisked off into a love story with a teenage Michael.

"Here it is," my grandmother said, walking back into the living room with an old spiral notebook in her hands. Running my fingers over the pages, it wasn't the words so much as the handwriting itself that got me. My mother wrote in a kind of hybrid cursive, a flowing script that reminded me of the sketches fashion designers use to plan their collections. Then I remembered the notes she'd put in my lunch box every day in elementary school. Short one- or two-sentence messages written in that flowing script. I always ate the dessert snack and threw away the sandwich, glaring at the lunch lady lording over the trash cans as she threatened to tell my mother. I couldn't remember what I did with those notes — if I shoved them into my pockets, if I dumped them in the trash too. Why hadn't I kept them? A good son would've kept them. I had so little of her handwriting left now.

Stop, I'd eventually have to tell myself,

just stop. I handed the notebook back to my grandmother. The past was a siren song, offering to give my mother back if I dared to make stories about her my sustenance. Whenever I tried, however, I quickly found myself dragged under by a riptide. A story became a memory became a guilt-laced question before finally, there at the bottom of the sea, I'd find the same fact waiting for me: I was never going to see her again. To avoid the lure of memories, I threw myself into the work of planning to bury her.

My uncle Albert is good with death. When my grandfather died, Albert guided my grandmother and the rest of the family through the countless decisions that have to be made in order to put a loved one to rest. Over the years, he had stepped into this role over and over again without complaint. Throughout the time my mother was in a coma and then, during the flurry of errands leading up to her funeral, my uncle was the easiest person for me to be with.

In a family of mostly women, I had never expected to be the kind of man who fled their company, relieved to just sit in silence with my uncle. He didn't ask how I felt, but he would hug me or put his hand on my shoulder at the precise moment I needed to be comforted, just before I realized it myself. He seemed to thrive on creating a sense of order, on understanding the tasks to be taken care of. We turned the dining room into a command center. Armed with yellow pads and lists of phone numbers, we took turns calling insurance companies and banks, deciding on fonts for the funeral program and guest lists. I would stay at that table, making phone calls and checking off "to do" items as late as he would let me.

After nearly a decade of barely speaking with him, I realized that my relationship with my uncle had somehow remained intact. Maybe this is why, in the depths of her unconscious fears, Mom had always called out for him in her sleep. She knew that he was steadfast. This was the uncle who, when I was eleven or twelve, took me aside and said, "In some tribes, when you turn thirteen, you are a real man. It's time to start thinking like a real man." As I was sitting cross-legged on a carpet littered with action figures, I realized what he said to me then had repulsed me. "Real men" scared me. I didn't want to be one. Now, in my midtwenties, planning my mother's funeral, I understood what he'd meant. It didn't matter whether "man" was the word best suited for who I had become. What mattered was the other word. I felt more real, more like myself, than I ever had before. There were no more masks left for me to hide behind.

Sitting in the passenger seat of his SUV as my uncle drove us to the grocery store, it occurred to me that we were now two of the oldest men in our immediate family. And then, somehow that thought led to another one so I spoke up.

"Uncle, I'm gay," I said, keeping my eyes on the road ahead of us. "I guess I've never actually said it to you."

"Oh, I know," he answered, his eyes also steady on the road. His tone wasn't dismissive or heavy; it was simply his, that calm directness that made it clear why he was so good at being the father of a large family, a deacon at his church, and a senior executive at his company.

"It doesn't really seem to matter much now, to be honest, but I just wanted to say it."

"Okay, nephew." He smiled. I went back to watching the trees blur as we sped past them.

At the grocery store, I held up two different packages of hot dog buns, trying to decide, while he picked up a bag of chips. When my uncle turned his back to me, I looked at him and then almost cried thinking of his smile.

When your mother is a single parent and you are her only child and she doesn't have a will, if she dies in the state of Tennessee, you are designated as the next of kin. I heard the term "next of kin" crackling on the other end of phone lines for weeks, then I started seeing "next of kin" on paperwork from lawyers, banks, clerk's offices, and the morgue. As next of kin, it had fallen to me, a few days before the funeral, to call the insurance company and tell the woman how much the ceremony we had planned would cost. She was only allowed to tell me whether the policy could cover that amount, and she said matter-of-factly that it could. I paused, hoping that she would at least give me a hint of whether we could afford a nicer funeral service — maybe the casket with rose-gold handles instead of brass, or a more extravagant floral arrangement? But the insurance agent answered my silence with a steelier silence and I finally said, "Thank you," and hung up.

I told my uncle that we were in the clear and immediately began to wonder about the number the woman must have been staring at on her computer screen. Was it too late to find out if I could buy my mother a designer gown to be buried in? It seemed cruel to have so little information on which to decide exactly how we would say goodbye to her. But I felt my uncle patting my shoulder with a light squeeze and tried to remember to be grateful. At least we weren't going into debt to give my mother a proper funeral.

The day before the service, standing in the funeral home's hallway, my uncle handed me his phone so I could plead with a florist to accept a last-minute order of sunflowers. "They were her favorite," I said. "She'd buy them at the grocery store when she could and keep them in a vase on the kitchen counter." I was ashamed at how quickly my voice would devolve into cracked stutters and babbled memories. "Can you do this for her, please?" The woman on the other end of the line, likely staring at an entire list of funeral arrangement orders, sighed and agreed.

We had a traditional Buddhist ceremony and then a secular service. The sunflowers calmed me, so I looked at them whenever I felt tears or memories begin to take hold. As we were chanting, I looked over at my grandmother. She kept her head bowed, perhaps praying her own prayers. I felt grateful, then, that she had allowed me —

and her daughter — this grace. Halfway through the service, one of my aunts sang "The Wind Beneath My Wings" to comfort my grandmother. My mother's best friend read Nikki Giovanni's poem "Ego Tripping (there may be a reason why)" at my request. After I finished chanting, I stared at the flowers until it was time for me to deliver the eulogy. I walked to the podium, looked at the crowded room, and started speaking. Like a prayer I'd been chanting day and night for weeks, I could feel the words leaving my mouth but I couldn't hear them.

At the cemetery, we stood under a white gazebo. I kept my eyes straight ahead and walked slowly, first behind my mother's casket, then behind my family as we left the casket behind. It was so bright outside, a spring day so beautiful it seemed rude given the circumstances. I followed my grandmother as we stepped out of the gazebo and into the sunlight. She had been mostly silent all day, but now she threw back her head. "My baby girl," she cried. "That was my baby girl." She had to lean on someone for support, but I can only picture who it wasn't.

20

June 2011
Jersey City, New Jersey

Back in Jersey City, I took a breath and reached into the mailbox. Lately, I'd been able to make it through most days at work without crying, but every time I got home I would find a pile of envelopes addressed to my mother, and the tears would have me gasping for air before I could make it inside my apartment.

This time, though, I found an envelope with an insurance company's logo on it addressed to me. I took a breath, then ripped it open, unfolding what turned out to be a life insurance statement. I started blinking, trying as best I could to see the number before the tears already pooling in my eyes rendered every digit a blur. I stepped into my building and held my hand over my mouth. The force of the scream made me double over as if I'd been punched in the

234

stomach. I'd been told to expect a check, but nothing could have prepared me for the amount printed on the dotted line.

A few months before she died, I had agonized over whether I could afford to give my mother the $800 she had asked for to help fix her car. I finally did after a coworker reminded me, "You only have one mother." My mother was gone now and, in her stead, I had a check worth more money than either of us had seen in our lives. A cruel joke. The overdrawn checking accounts for the sake of groceries and heart medication. The doctors' and dentists' visits put off for too long.

Though for years at that point I'd thought of her failing health as inevitable, staring at the number on the paper in my hand I saw that a different story had once been possible. It wasn't always necessarily going to end this way. If she hadn't been living paycheck to paycheck, maybe she would not have needed to smoke so heavily to deal with her stress. Maybe there had been earlier avenues of treatment that would've spared her congestive heart failure in the first place. Maybe she could have been able to go back to school, gotten her college degree. What if, what if, what if . . .

I couldn't tell which hurt more: the onslaught of ideas about what could have been, or all the memories I had of what actually happened. My mother crying in front of her altar because she couldn't afford to send me to NYU. My mother sitting across from a banker who had denied her for yet another loan. My mother pacing in line at the grocery store, hoping her debit card wouldn't be declined.

And now this check was in my hand, bought and paid for with her life.

I climbed the steps to my apartment and slid back down to my knees once I was in the kitchen. We could've had more flowers at her funeral. We could've decided on the casket with the rose-gold handles. We could've buried her in a designer gown with diamond rings on every finger and black pearls around her neck. Instead, my mother would wear the suit her sister picked out for her until the fabric disintegrated and succumbed to the dirt and worms. My ears rang with everything we could've done, everything we could no longer do. I would never get to bury her again.

21

September 2011
Barcelona, Spain

I cleaned out my mother's apartment that summer. Next to her altar, I found a note card she'd been keeping with a list of what she called determinations. At the bottom was this: "I will travel and see the world with my son."

We never got the chance. But I went without her as summer faded, feeling untethered, like a wheel without an axle. I floated through one town to the next, winding my way through western Europe. Each morning I woke up wondering where I was, grasping at the last ray of a dream about my mother, even as the details turned to ash.

One morning, I leaned over the edge of my bed and nearly tumbled out, realizing only then that I was on the top of a bunk bed. I craned my neck to look at the bed under me and saw a blonde girl snoring softly. The night before we'd gone on a pub crawl together along Las Ramblas. This was Barcelona. I was in a hostel in Barcelona. Not Jersey City, not Memphis, not Lewisville.

I was pouring myself some cereal for breakfast when I noticed an older lady in the hostel's common area. Most of the guests in the hostel were in their early twenties. Australians, forever on vacation, it seemed. Americans doing a gap year, backpacking across Europe. Young couples on their honeymoon. Quiet young women getting over breakups. This woman looked to be in her sixties, small but spry. Tourists like her usually seemed to travel in packs, but she stuck out. I ate my cereal, trying not to stare at her from across the room, wondering what this woman was doing alone in Spain.

After breakfast, I'd only made it a few blocks before I had to go back to the hostel to get the wallet I had forgotten in my room. When I came back downstairs, the older woman was standing by the front door, about to head out into the day herself. She happened to be holding a brochure for the Picasso Museum, exactly where I was going. I'd been keeping to myself, avoiding talking to other hostel guests as much as possible, but I felt like I should say something.

"Oh, I'm going to that museum too," I said.

"Really?" Her voice sounded like a parody of an old lady's voice, a young person's idea of what a silver-haired white lady would sound like, except it had such force. Her words shot out. "Well, we should go together. I'm Esther." She took my hand and shook it. Again, such force. I tried not to wince.

Though I hadn't really planned on us spending our time at the museum *together,* once we were there, instead of going our separate ways, Esther and I made small talk. We walked from room to room, looking at paintings and sketches, trying to make sense of the descriptions written in Spanish and Catalan, talking about the hostels we'd seen throughout Europe.

"I tried one of those bus trips with other retirees," she said at one point, "but old people are so . . . old." Esther giggled at her own cleverness and I laughed too. She told me she was a retired nurse from Ontario who'd found she loved traveling overseas by herself. When she asked me what I was doing in Spain, I just said that I was writing, looking for material. Part of the relief of traveling alone was that I didn't have to talk about my mother. As I strolled through Barcelona, though, she was all I thought about.

At the gift shop, Esther bought several postcards — not for grandchildren, as I had expected, but for the policeman she had recently started dating. Every time she turned away from me, it seemed, I caught myself staring at the curious marvel of this fierce little woman. She didn't ask if I wanted to go to lunch with her; we just went to lunch. While we waited for our food, I asked about the other trips she had taken alone.

"Well, last summer I visited all the Holocaust museums and memorials."

"Wait. *All?*"

"Every single one in Europe. Took me all summer," she explained, smiling broadly. In the glint of her eyes, I could tell that I was giving her that baffled stare again.

"Are you Jewish?"

"No. I just . . . oh, I don't know." She paused. "I was just curious about how one man could get so many people to do something so awful."

As the day went on, we stuck together, drifting from cathedral to cathedral, monument to monument. Esther refused to take taxis, even as I dragged behind her, whining and sweating. At one point, as we walked down an interminably long city block that may have been uphill, or simply seemed that way because of the late-summer heat, I watched Esther plowing ahead as I walked behind her. I would've laughed if I hadn't been so tired. Why was I following this little old white lady all over Barcelona? Why was I in Barcelona in the first place? The questions shimmered in the air like the heat.

A month after the funeral, I had woken up in my apartment in Jersey City and looked around the room. I realized I couldn't do it anymore. I needed to wake up somewhere new; I needed everything I saw as soon as I opened my eyes to say clearly and definitely that my life had changed. Too much had happened for me to keep waking up surrounded by the lie of continuity. I had already decided that when the school year ended, I wouldn't return to teach again. Trying to take care of those kids when I was barely taking care of myself just didn't seem right. And, when I was seized by the fog of grief, writing brought me the kind of clarity that I desperately needed.

I moved to a one-bedroom apartment in Harlem that cost twice as much as my previous studio. *I can afford this now because my mother is dead. I'm a poet living in Harlem now because my mother is dead. My full-time job is writing now because my mother is dead.* I couldn't separate the monstrous from the miraculous. Friends would try to convince me otherwise, framing her sacrifice as a gift my mother had given me, but I wasn't so sure. It felt cruel to mine personal meaning out of her death. I didn't want to redefine her life and death as a journey toward sacrifice. It's *still* difficult, at times, to talk about my mother without inadvertently rendering her as a beautiful stone idol. Sometimes I hear a voice in my head asking, "Who died and made you king?"

The next day, Esther and I went to the beach with some of the other people from the hostel. We stopped at a bodega along the way and got several bottles of sangria.

"Did you know all this sand was imported from Egypt?" said Esther as we spread out our towels on the white sandy beach. I smiled and shrugged. "The country had all the sand shipped in to make the beaches look prettier when they hosted the Olympics. I think palm trees too." We looked at a nearby tree, as if we were natives eyeing an interloper in our midst. Esther and I toasted our bottles of sangria.

As Esther played with the sand next to her, combing it with her wrinkled fingers, I thought about my grandmother, who must've been just a few years older than Esther. She had never been to Europe. I couldn't remember the last time I had chatted with her as easily as I did with Esther. My grandmother and I didn't *chat;* that was never our relationship. But we had, in the months after Mom died, started calling each other again. The calls were short, and we rarely if ever talked about Mom. Yet her presence was always there somehow. Early in the summer, I was calling from my new apartment in Harlem, and just as we reached the lull in the conversation that usually precipitated us ending the call, my grandmother let out a heavy sigh.

"I sure do miss that woman," she said.

It's difficult to describe the warmth I felt in her voice right then. I could hear my grandmother smiling on the other end of the line, as an image of her daughter formed in her mind: Carol Jean smiling in the sunlight, sunglasses on, hair shimmering. *That woman.* I heard my grandmother's joy build, and I heard grief come back to snatch her smile away. Good memories had become self-inflicted cruelties for us.

It knocked the wind out of me. I hunched

my shoulders and nodded, unable to answer her back. I'd heard so many people speak lovingly of my mother since she died, but no sentence had as much love tucked into it as my grandmother's "I sure do miss that woman." For the first time in years I wished I could hug — really hug — my grandmother. I wished Mom could have heard the love in her mother's voice just then.

As Esther lounged, I decided to go for a swim. The ocean was a bright shade of blue, with swirls of emerald springing forth when the light hit the waves just right.

When I first stepped into the water, I almost laughed. At its warmth, like an embrace. The tease of waves licking my ankles. The shock of coming into contact with a body of water that vast, then vanishing into it.

I drifted out into waves the color of peacock feathers. They pulled me away from shore, and into a dream I'd had about my mother earlier that summer. We had been driving across one of the old bridges in Bowling Green, me at the wheel and Mom in the passenger seat. It was a bright, cloudless afternoon. Music played on the radio and we had our windows rolled down, so my mother kept waving her hair out of her face. We laughed, or at least I heard laughter. We had been driving across the bridge all day, but my mother didn't seem to notice. She kept waving strands of hair out of her eyes and switching radio stations. The bridge just kept going, mile after mile. It irritated me that Mom hadn't realized. With one hand still on the wheel, I reached over and touched her hand.

I put my hand back on the wheel, but the skin where I had touched her turned an iridescent blue, tinged with green. A peacock stain soon marked her hand and we stared at each other. Somehow, this was how we knew she was dying. She tried to apologize, but I only looked back at the road ahead and pressed down on the gas. The bridge stretched out and out.

A blink and we were in a white-tiled bathroom, both of us standing in the empty bathtub. The peacock stain had spread from her hand to the rest of her arm. "I'm sorry," she said again. But something unsettled in me. I don't know why, but I grabbed her by the collar of her shirt. I shoved her against the wall. I held her there as she cried, and I cursed at her.

This had been my first dream about my mother since her funeral. Gasping, I woke in my apartment in Harlem. A bright, cloudless morning, just like on the bridge. My sobs were so violent, my ribs hurt. For months, I had been waiting, hoping, for her to appear in my dreams. I thought she would answer some questions, or just sit beside me, but instead, when she finally showed up, I hurt her. Every time I squeezed my eyes shut, I could still see her pressed against the tile wall, struggling to keep her balance in the tub, her shirt collar still in my grip, her eyes locked on mine as she cried.

I knew where this part of the dream came from. One morning during my junior year of high school, an unspoken argument between us finally broke open. I can't even remember why we were arguing, but I remember growling: "I love you so much. You're the best mother anyone could want." I injected my voice with as much venom as I could muster, and I said it over and over. With each repetition, she slapped me. *I love you so much.* Slap. *You're the best mother anyone could want.* Slap. I kept going until my eyes shined, until I was screaming.

My mother, several inches shorter than me, grabbed the collar of my shirt and pinned me against the sliding glass door of the patio. I remember feeling myself lifted onto the tips of my toes. My voice was hoarse and my mother was so livid she sounded otherworldly. We shouted back and forth, neither hearing a single word, until we were both exhausted. When she let go, I ran out of the apartment.

Like the actual impetus for the fight, whatever happened next is a blank. All that remains is the single ugliest moment between the two of us. My mother and I at our worst.

That is the memory that came hurtling toward me when I woke up from the dream in Harlem. I was shaken, terrified that this is what all dreams about my mother would be like. Brutal memories, distorted and looped.

I love you so much. You're the best mother anyone could want. I'm almost certain I said those exact sentences while holding my mother's hand in the ICU.

I was shocked by how vivid it seemed. The memory of her death came surging forth again, as if I'd been in the hospital with her just the day before.

Would it always be this way? Time cascading and crashing in on itself, each memory pushing me back toward the beginning of my grief. I didn't know if I could take it.

I realized, as I swam out farther than I'd expected, that I was sobbing. The tears ripped through me as I treaded water. I tried to stay above the waves, but they kept breaking against my neck and face. I was exhausted. My body, my mind. My life itself felt exhausted. I started swimming back to shore but the waves resisted me. Drunk on sangria, tired from the sunshine and the crying, I started slipping under the surf. Water went up my nose, into my mouth. I coughed, sputtered, started swimming again, struggling to keep my head above water. Wave after wave kept coming in.

My arms and legs were so heavy. Maybe I had fought long enough. Maybe I could just let go, stop fighting, and ease down into the sea. I thought it over, paddling and paddling. I decided, "Yes, I will let go."

I stopped kicking my legs. I stopped stroking my arms against the sea. I started to sink and let the water crest over my head. I let a last breath escape my lungs. And just then, the tips of my toes brushed against sand.

The waves had pushed me back toward the beach; I hadn't even noticed. The peacock blue had saved me from myself.

I let out a small laugh. I felt the sand under my feet. I felt the waves tugging me back toward shore. The ocean shimmered around me. She would have loved this place,

I knew. *I wish she could see it,* I thought. Then, *I guess I'm seeing it for us.*

I made my way out of the water and back to Esther and the rest of our new friends. I sat down and she handed me a bottle of sangria.

"It's a little warm," she said.

Our last night together in Barcelona, Esther and I went out for dinner. We ordered tapas and giggled every time she said "sangrita," even though she already knew it was called "sangria." The café we chose was in an outdoor plaza overlooking the city. In an easy silence, we watched the sunset together.

"My mother died in May. That's why I'm here," I said, finally, still looking ahead.

"My mother died this year too."

I wonder if we had, in some way, always known that we had this in common.

Holding hands across the table, we took turns letting the words pour out of us. It was overwhelming, describing the women we missed so much. Words coming home like waves. It was freeing to just say it.

Our mothers are why we are here.

ACKNOWLEDGMENTS

My literary agent, Charlotte Sheedy, has had faith in me from the beginning. Her support ensured that I was able to write this book under the best possible circumstances. Equally important, Jonathan Cox — my patient, lovely editor at Simon & Schuster — is simply one of the most brilliant people I have ever gotten to work alongside. He has been my champion and lodestar throughout this process. Thank you to the many, many people at Simon & Schuster who have contributed to this book's journey. Thank you to the wonderful folks at The Tuesday Agency. Thank you, Sam Hall and Karisma Price.

Thank you to my grandmother and the rest of my family for trusting me to tell my truth as best I could. Thank you, Aunt Janet; I love you more than the air I breathe. Thank you to my chosen family for reminding me again and again that, though the work was daunting, I was never alone. Isaac Fitzgerald. Ellen Claycomb. Lukas Thoms. Christopher Jerrolds. Teddy Goff. Marc Dones. Marlon James. David Speer. Adam Ellis. Benj Pasek. Rachel Kaadzi Ghansah. Angel Nafis. Morgan Parker. Danez Smith. Kiese Laymon. Syreeta McFadden. Adam Falkner. Alexander Chee.

Thank you to my therapist, David Witten.

Thank you, Sarah Schulman, for being the earliest reader of what would become chapters of this book.

Thank you to my mentors: Rigoberto Gonzalez. Tayari Jones. Patricia Smith. Roxane Gay. Ben Smith. Shani Hilton. Sally Squibb. Kelly Reames. Tom Hunley.

ABOUT THE AUTHOR

Saeed Jones is the author of *Prelude to Bruise,* winner of the 2015 PEN/Joyce Osterweil Award for Poetry and the 2015 Stonewall Book Award-Barbara Gittings Literature Award. The poetry collection was also a finalist for the 2014 National Book Critics Circle Award, as well as awards from Lambda Literary and the Publishing Triangle in 2015. Jones is a former cohost of the BuzzFeed News morning show, *@AM2DM,* and previously served as BuzzFeed's LGBT editor and culture editor. Jones was born in Memphis, Tennessee, and grew up in Lewisville, Texas. He earned a BA at Western Kentucky University and an MFA at Rutgers University–Newark. He tweets @TheFerocity.

The employees of Thorndike Press hope you have enjoyed this Large Print book. All our Thorndike, Wheeler, and Kennebec Large Print titles are designed for easy reading, and all our books are made to last. Other Thorndike Press Large Print books are available at your library, through selected bookstores, or directly from us.

For information about titles, please call:
(800) 223-1244

or visit our website at:
gale.com/thorndike

To share your comments, please write:
Publisher
Thorndike Press
10 Water St., Suite 310
Waterville, ME 04901